POLITICAL OPINION
IN MASSACHUSETTS DURING CIVIL
WAR AND RECONSTRUCTION

BY

EDITH ELLEN WARE

AMS PRESS
NEW YORK

COLUMBIA UNIVERSITY
STUDIES IN THE
SOCIAL SCIENCES

175

The Series was formerly known as
Studies in History, Economics and Public Law.

Reprinted with the permission of Columbia University Press
From the edition of 1916, New York
First AMS EDITION published 1968
Manufactured in the United States of America

Library of Congress Catalogue Card Number: 77-76697

AMS PRESS, INC.
NEW YORK, N. Y. 10003

PREFACE

In the following pages no attempt has been made to re-write the story of the Civil War, nor has there been any effort to narrate the steps of Reconstruction; that has been ably done from various points of view. This monograph presupposes that such works are very familiar and confines itself, as its title indicates, to the political opinion within a single state during those critical years. Massachusetts is inevitably prominent in the history of that time. She was one of the larger states and had an active aggressive governor; many of her citizens were in positions of national importance. In fact Robert C. Winthrop complained:

I cannot but regret that our state is put forward so prominently. Sumner at the head of Foreign Affairs, Wilson at the head of Military Affairs, Butler commanding one wing, Banks commanding another wing, Adams Minister to London, Burlingame to Pekin, Motley to Vienna, Regiment after Regiment of Massa&c volunteers hurrying to the conflict—all this tends to keep up the idea that this is a Mass(&c) War and provokes increased hostility and exasperation at the South.[1]

Aside from this political prestige it should be noted that abolitionist propaganda centered in Boston, and that its great leaders and influential sympathizers were citizens of Massachusetts whose activity colored the contemporary opinion of her held by outsiders and has continued to color the memory of her attitude even to the present (1916). Furthermore the eastern part of the state was the home of

[1] *Winthrop MSS*, to Judge Clifford, Aug. 24, 1861.

prominent literary men of the period, and, although the extent of the influence of their presence and opinion on the political situation may be questioned, their general anti-slavery attitude is well known and together with the abolitionist agitation is best remembered as the opinion of Massachusetts.

By reputation the Bay State has always been Republican. But a majority never expresses the whole political opinion. Besides it is a minority which at times makes itself most felt, as for example, in national affairs, in the Civil War itself. The position and character of a minority is often forgotten; for history records merely the success of the triumphant, and tradition passes on the thoughts of the conspicuous. I purpose here to inquire into the strength of the minority, and the reasons for their opposition and their strength; to discover who were the spectacular and famous individuals or representatives of both sides; and to ascertain what the majority really thought. In other words, I shall try to present a comprehensive study of the political opinion in Massachusetts during the Civil War and Reconstruction.

The material for the present work has been gathered largely from newspaper files, chiefly those of the Boston and Springfield Public Libraries and the Antiquarian Society at Worcester. Collections of pamphlets and broadsides which are in the rooms of the Massachusetts Historical Society and the State Library [1] were consulted and in addition such private papers as were available. I wish to express my indebtedness to attendants of these libraries, as well as to the librarians of Columbia and Harvard Universities and Smith College, of Peabody Institute in Baltimore, and of the Clarke and the Forbes Libraries in Northampton. I

---

[1] Fuller accounts of this material will be found in appendices ii and iii.

have also received material through personal channels, chiefly in the form of suggestions and reminiscences.   I am indebted especially to Mrs. Sarah Hughes of Milton, daughter of John Murray Forbes; to Professor Henry Greenleaf Pearson of the Institute of Technology; to Dr. Worthington C. Ford and to the late Dr. Samuel A. Green of the Massachusetts Historical Society; to Mr. Frank B. Sanborn and Colonel N. P. Hallowell, and also to the late Miss Ann Page and neighbors of Danvers, and to residents of Worcester, of the neighborhood of Bridgewater, Plymouth County, and to yet others of the Hadleys.

Finally I owe grateful acknowledgment in particular to Professor John Spencer Bassett of Smith College, who suggested the line of investigation, and to Professor William A. Dunning, who has encouraged the work to its completion.

EDITH ELLEN WARE.

NORTHAMPTON, 1916.

CONTENTS

CHAPTER V

THE RISE AND FALL OF COPPERHEADISM

CHAPTER VI

PART I

RECONSTRUCTION—THEORIES AND POLICIES

PART 2

POLITICAL ISSUES TO 1876

INTRODUCTION

THE records of anti-slavery agitation incident to the Compromise of 1850, written, for the most part, by the friends or champions of freedom, give the impression that all of Massachusetts, conscious of the crime of American slavery, was determined to be rid of it. This is not the fact of the case. The Free-Soilers were actually in the minority throughout the decade preceding Republican dominance; but although limited in numbers, they were unlimited in determination and ability. They could not win of themselves, therefore they won by coalition. But win they did, and the success of the minority has given the impression that it was the will of the majority.

The Free-Soil party was organized in the state in 1848. In 1850 it took advantage of the disaffection among the Whigs which followed Webster's " Seventh of March speech ", and joining with the Democrats replaced the dominant Whig party. This coalition failed to win the majority necessary for the choice of governor, but it controlled the legislature in both 1851 and 1852. And the coalition legislature named a Free-Soiler to uphold anti-slavery measures in Congress, namely, Charles Sumner for the long-term senatorship, and Henry Wilson for president of the state senate; it elected George S. Boutwell, then a Democrat, for governor and appointed Democrats to the short-term senatorship and the speakership of the legislature. Thus through controlling the coalition the Free-Soilers put forward men who continued to lead and to personify the extreme anti-slavery factions of the state. But such a coalition could not last; the presidential campaign of 1852 clearly defined party principles, and the Kansas-Nebraska bill of 1854 ended all compromise.

In consequence of this definition of parties the Whigs came into power once more, in 1853. They had polled a plurality of the popular vote during the years of the coalition, but had failed to elect their candidate for governor because a majority was necessary. After 1854 they failed to have either a majority or a plurality. The clearly defined issue which put an end to the coalition of 1851 and 1852 was also dividing the Whig party. In the heightening contest with the Southern advocates of slavery, those following the leadership of Webster believed any compromise was justifiable which would preserve the Union; Rufus Choate, for example, argued that to return a few fugitives was better than to sacrifice multitudes in civil strife. Representative leaders of the Whig party were willing if need be to submit to the complete nationalization of slavery as the lesser of the two evils.[1] Many " Conscience Whigs ", however, in distinction from " Cotton Whigs ", were unwilling to yield everything to one idea. This controversy ended in the weakening and final breaking-up of the Whig party.

The episode of the " Know-Nothings " occurring at this juncture, superficially diverted attention from the paramount issue. This party arose in protest against the multitude of immigrants, Irish Catholic in particular, that had recently come to Massachusetts. The increase in the percentage of illiterates, dependents and criminals from this element of the population was out of all proportion to their numbers, and contributed much to the burdens of the substantial people of the state. Moreover, the number of foreigners eager for activity in politics alarmed the people generally lest, subject to

---

[1] *Cf.* C. F. Adams, *Life of C. F. Adams*, ch. iv: The " Boston Whig."

the will of a foreign potentate, these strangers should subvert America's civil and religious liberties. Consequently the secret organizations against the invaders grew apace, and, combined in the general organization of the American party,[1] they soon nominated and elected their candidates to public office. On the slavery question the new party professed a neutral stand. This, since it was what the Democrats were contending for, satisfied those among them who desired to join the anti-foreign crusade. Neutrality on the slavery question appealed especially to the Whigs also, since they were at odds among themselves upon that issue. Accordingly analysis of the vote of 1853 and 1854 seems to indicate that something like 55 per cent of the Whigs and 62 per cent of the Democrats deserted their old allegiance and that 77 per cent of the Free-Soilers merged themselves into the new party.[2] The Know-Nothings swept the state.

But here again the Free-Soilers were manipulating politics, here again they were using coalition. It was necessary to the cause of the Free-Soilers to break down the old parties. They therefore joined the new party in order to defeat the old. But they did more: they used the new mechanism to serve their cause. Henry Wilson, in retrospect, said of the party that

hundreds of thousands who cared less for its avowed principles and purposes than for the higher claims of justice and humanity, and had little faith in its permanency, were willing to use its machinery to disrupt the Whig and Democratic parties in the confident hope that, out of the disorganized

[1] The nickname "Know-Nothing" is used interchangeably with American.

[2] G. H. Haynes, "A Know-Nothing Legislature," in American Historical Association, *Report*, 1896, p. 180. The composition and work of this legislature is admirably analyzed in this article.

masses, there would come a great political party antagonistic to the dominating influences of the Slave Power.[1]

This is undoubtedly what resulted. The Know-Nothing members of the legislature were inexperienced and the Free-Soilers among them directed its work to their ends. Henry Wilson was elected senator; seven out of eleven congressmen, nominally Know-Nothing, were Free-Soilers, and all were understood to be anti-slavery in sympathy. Free-Soil sentiment was also shown in the passage of the Personal Liberty Bill and in an address to the governor demanding the removal of Judge Loring who, as United States commissioner, had rendered a decision obnoxious to Massachusetts anti-slavery sentiment. The only real Know-Nothing legislation was the proposal of an amendment to the state constitution restricting office-holding to native born and the franchise to residents of twenty-one years.[2]

The year of the Know-Nothing landslide (1854) also witnessed the ineffectual effort to organize a Republican party. The Whigs, in control in 1853, still held the hope of continued power, and added an anti-slavery plank to their platform. The Know-Nothing candidate, a former conservative Whig, was said to be anti-slavery; the Free-Soil party satisfied the more extreme champions of freedom. All the parties excepting the pronounced Democrats were thus opposed to the repeal of the Missouri Compromise; yet only one party, the Free-Soil, was willing to place that question above all else, and slavery in the territories could not therefore be made an issue. The people generally, in fact, were not yet ready to join a party dominated by Free-Soilers, as the organizing Republican party appeared to be.[3] The contest consequently

---

[1] Wilson, *Rise and Fall of the Slave Power*, vol. ii, p. 49.
[2] This amendment was defeated in the next legislature.
[3] Wilson, *op. cit.*, vol. ii, p. 414.

was between the Whigs and the Know-Nothings. And the Know-Nothing party, victorious in its first campaign, gained momentum enough to reëlect its governor in 1855.

The landslide that buried the old parties was itself soon turned aside. At the national convention in Philadelphia in 1855 the Know-Nothing party divided on its declaration of principles. The committee on resolutions reported, fourteen to thirteen, that congress ought not to prohibit slavery in any territory or in the District of Columbia, and that it had no power to exclude any state from admission to the Union because its constitution recognized slavery. The minority demanded a restoration of the Missouri Compromise line, or, failing that, refusal on the part of Congress to admit any state formed out of the Kansas-Nebraska territories which tolerated slavery. The debate continued for three days. The Northern delegates were well satisfied with all planks but the one on slavery. On that point the Know-Nothings as a national party were rent in twain. Anti-slavery sentiment had always been strong in the Know-Nothing party in the North, and when the party was shorn of its secrecy during and after the convention of 1855 and when it was forced into an open statement of its principles, the slavery question came to the fore. In Massachusetts the disintegrating American party took the same position on the slavery question as the newly organizing Republican party, and for the year, 1855, maintained itself in power.

The Republican party, organized in 1855, was under the leadership of Samuel Bowles, E. Rockwood Hoar, Richard Henry Dana, Jr., Charles Francis Adams, George S. Boutwell and Henry L. Dawes. A conference committee of all parties was held and a state convention was called to meet in Worcester, September 20, 1855. There Nathaniel P. Banks, (coalition Democrat of 1851) presided and Richard H. Dana, Jr., (Free-Soiler) was chairman of the platform committee. The nomination for governor was a subject of much debate. The alliance of the Americans depended upon the nomination of Gardner; the party in power was not willing to resign to a new party. The Republicans, however, nominated their own candidate, Julius Rockwell. Rockwell and Beach (the Democratic nominee) represented the two sides of the great question. But the Americans had accepted the anti-slavery issue, thus preventing deflection to the new party, and Gardner, backed by the organization and prestige of the previous year's victory, was elected. Thus for the second time the new Republican party failed: in 1854 to organize, in 1855 to elect its candidate.

In the presidential year 1856 the Americans still held to their organization. But since a large proportion of them did not differ from the Republicans on the main issue, the new party used coalition as had the Free-Soilers on former occasions. Desiring to obtain united support for Fremont, the Republicans agreed to put up no candidate against Gardner, the representative of American dominance in the state. The American party, however, was not yet merely an anti-slavery party; there were some who still adhered to the original tenets, but were opposed to Fremont. They therefore organized as Fillmore-Americans. In the election Massachusetts voted for a Republican president and a Fremont-American governor.

But the union of Republican and American parties on the main issue permanently weakened the latter as an independent party, and in 1857 the Fremont Americans joined with the Republicans in electing Nathaniel P. Banks and a Republican legislature. The national problem of slavery in the territories had usurped the place of all other interests, and the national party founded on that issue alone had diverted attention from all other causes. Banks and the Republican legislature were retained in power.

The Whigs made no nominations after 1856, the American party grew smaller and smaller, disappearing in 1860. And the Free-Soilers, having failed utterly to grow, again exercised their influence in coalition: they became merged in the more moderate Republican party.

In 1860, therefore, the Democratic party was the lone party left, from those of the previous decade, to oppose the Republicans. Having broken with the Free-Soilers in 1853 and having championed popular sovereignty and non-interference with slavery in the territories, it had, like the Republican party, drawn unto itself members of the other groups who had deserted minor causes for the paramount issue.

Consequently our point of departure for the discussion of the Political Opinion in Massachusetts during the Civil War and Reconstruction is an analysis of the parties and votes in the campaign of 1860.

CHAPTER I

THE ELECTION OF 1860

ON January 25, 1860, Henry Wilson, in the United States Senate, made a long and carefully prepared speech, which was an enunciation of the purposes and principles of the Republican party in the campaign about to begin. Throwing aside the doctrines of the extreme Abolitionists, he was content to rest the issue of the campaign on the question of the exclusion of slavery from the territories. It was the object of the party, he said,

to preserve the vast territorial possessions of the Republic from " the direful effects " of this " dreadful calamity " which " has preyed upon the vitals of the Union ", by applying to, and engraving upon, those territorial possessions these words, " *slavery shall* BE AND IS FOREVER *prohibited* "; words which came from the pen of Jefferson, were embodied in the Ordinance of 1787, and stamped on every foot of the virgin sods of the Northwest.[1]

This was commended as a " full, free and frank declaration of the principles and purposes of the North," [2] and it was echoed, in a somewhat softer tone, by the platform of the Massachusetts Republicans. That instrument

[1] *Cong. Globe*, 36 cong., 1 sess., p. 571.

[2] Springfield *Republican*, Jan. 26, 1860. Throughout the year various newspapers continually referred to this speech as the standard of the party.

was written with a view of winning the conservative vote.
While it surrendered nothing of the principle that the
territories be devoted to free labor, it declared that it did
not contemplate the overthrow of slavery, nor ask the
suffrage of the people that it might oppress or wrong any
section, South or North; but it declared that the Republican
party was a union party, standing on the principles of the
fathers, who made freedom national and slavery sectional,
and that those men were sectional who stood for or against
slavery in the abstract.[1]

This principle of free territory swept so many of the
anti-slavery champions into the Republican party that the
conservative phraseology of the platform did not avert a
storm of denunciation from the opponents of the party.
The Republicans, said the opposition papers, were not entitled to be known as unionists.   Had their allies not long
preached, " No Union with Slaveholders "?   Had not the
arch-abolitionist announced that " the Constitution was a
Covenant with Death and an Agreement with Hell "?
Republicanism, the Democratic press dogmatically declared,
was nothing but open and undisguised abolitionism.   They
quoted Sumner's speech, of June 4, 1860, on the " Barbar-
ism of Slavery ", as the standard of the party; they claimed,
also, that Republican leaders had aided John Brown, and
they made capital of John A. Andrew's remark, " John
Brown himself was right ".   Thus they tried to make
the issue union or abolition, knowing that such an issue
would mean defeat to the Republicans, for Massachusetts,
however anti-slavery, was not abolitionist in sentiment.[2]

[1] Boston *Advertiser*, Aug. 30, 1860; Worcester *Spy*, Aug. 31, 1860.

[2] Fuller discussion of Massachusetts' attitude toward the abolition of
slavery will be found, *infra*, ch. iv.   The Boston *Post*, Apr. 9, 1869,
acknowledged the Abolitionists to be in the minority, but claimed that
by intellectual force they controlled the majority.

The Republican press, in point of fact, made emphatic protests against all imputation of abolitionism; even the most strongly anti-slavery paper, the *Atlas and Bee*,[1] declared angrily:

No man knows better than the editor of the *Post*, that the opinions entertained of old by Jews and Samaritans were not more wide apart than are the opinions held at the present time by the Republicans and the Garrisonian Abolitionists. The Republicans believe the Constitution of the United States to be an Antislavery document, and they bind themselves by their actions at the polls and by their oaths of office, and by the entire tenure of their political lives, to support and maintain it. The Garrisonian Abolitionists, on the other hand, believe the Constitution to be a proslavery document, and the Union to be a curse—and therefore they will not support the one and labor to destroy the other. They are non-voting men, and they will not accept office under the Constitution. Now then, we ask, can a man be a Republican, and at the same time a Garrisonian Abolitionist?

Moreover the distinction was emphasized by William Lloyd Garrison's Fourth-of-July speech:

The Republican party means to do nothing, can do nothing, for the abolition of slavery in the slave states. . . . The Republican party stands on a level with the Fugitive Slave Law. It has cursed all opposition to it . . . And shall I vote that men who buy and sell and steal their fellow creatures shall have political power put into their hands? . . . No . . . I am for meddling with slavery everywhere . . . in order to effect its eternal overthrow. . . . Excelsior! will be my cry . . . "*No Union* WITH SLAVE HOLDERS!" Down with this

---

[1] A characterization of Massachusetts newspapers for this period will be found in appendix ii. The newspapers referred to in the footnotes may be understood to be Boston publications unless otherwise designated.

slaveholding government! Let this "covenant with death and agreement with hell" be annulled![1]

Two events had, undoubtedly, given substance to Democratic accusations; namely, the support given to Sumner in 1856, and the raid of John Brown, friend of many Massachusetts Republicans. The truth of the matter, however, in the first instance, is that the reëlection of Sumner in 1856 was due less to his anti-slavery ideals than to a feeling of personal loyalty to a representative from Massachusetts who had received injury while serving his state. In the second instance, the John Brown affair was proved, in course of time, by a Senate report,[2] not to have been the will of the Republican party *per se*. Moreover it occurred long enough before the election for sober judgment in Massachusetts to correct charges[3] and to remove suspicions of possible guilt of Republicans in general, whatever share some individuals may have had in furnishing John Brown

[1] *Liberator*, July 20, 1860.

[2] This was the "Report of the Select Committee of the Senate appointed to inquire into the late invasion and seizure of the public property at Harper's Ferry," *Senate Reports*, 35 cong., 1 sess., vol. ii, no. 278. The committee was appointed at the instance of James M. Mason, of Virginia. *Globe*, 36 cong., 1 sess., pp. 1 and 52.

[3] *Advertiser*, Feb. 24, 1860: "The excitement about John Brown's invasion was out of proportion to the original occurrence and could not have arisen from it except by constant insistence from a partisan press." *Ibid.*, June 19, 1860: "If it had occurred a few months earlier it might have borne heavily upon the elections. But a political cry of this kind cannot last twelve months." Yet these statements are not true concerning the formation of the national party platforms. There, as Professor Fite states (*Campaign of 1860*, p. 32), the John Brown affair "forced the political parties of the country to assume extreme positions and declare extreme principles." This difference in effect upon national and state opinion is possible because the nominating conventions met in the spring, many weeks nearer the Harper's Ferry episode.

with funds, and it therefore proved useless as political capital. The Democratic accusations had greater effect within the South, especially in fostering the general opinion that a widespread abolition sentiment existed in Massachusetts in 1860.

But the real character of that anti-slavery sentiment which did exist was probably best expressed by the conservative *Republican* in its defense against Democratic misrepresentation. It explained at length that while the Republican party had no intention of interfering with the institution of slavery within the states, the party in Virginia might organize for emancipation of the slaves in Virginia; "But," it declared emphatically, "it is not legitimate to organize a Republican party in Massachusetts for the overthrow of slavery in Virginia. The United States cannot do it." It added that the only means the North could use was moral suasion.[1]

The campaign of 1860 began early. On March 7 the Massachusetts Republicans met to appoint delegates to the national convention. Although the appointees were not instructed the large majority were believed to favor the nomination of Seward.[2] At Chicago they so voted,— twenty-one out of twenty-six on the first ballot, twenty-two on the second, voted for Seward, and eighteen remained loyal on the third. But when the nomination of Lincoln was assured, ten more Massachusetts votes were transferred to him, totaling eighteen out of twenty-six. Then Andrew,

[1] Springfield *Republican*, Feb. 4, 1860, also Aug. 4, 1860.

[2] *Ibid.*, March 10, 1860; Worcester *Spy*, April 19, 1860; also Charles Eliot Norton to James Russell Lowell, Oct. 14, 1858; and Pearson, *Life of Andrew*, vol. i, p. 112. The minority of the delegates, George S. Boutwell and Linius B. Commins, were said (by both *Advertiser* and *Post*, March 8, 1860) to favor Nathaniel Banks, who had been Republican governor of Massachusetts 1857-1860.

chairman of the delegation, made a speech seconding
Evarts' motion for a unanimous nomination.[1]

On returning from the convention, J. W. Baldwin thought
it necessary to explain to the Worcester ratification meeting
that the nomination of Lincoln was the strongest that could
have been made under the circumstances.[2] Andrew, however, carried the Faneuil Hall meeting with him in enthusiastic endorsement of their candidate:

Men and brethren [he said] a greater than the battle of
Lundy's Lane lies before you. A higher duty falls now upon the
shoulders of the republicans of America than rested upon the
soldiers of 1814. It is for you to rescue from misgovernment
a country whose liberties were won by the blood of the Revolution. . . . It is for you to save and preserve that glorious
heritage which their valor won. The safety and peace of the
Republic and of the States, the preservation of the Constitution, the perpetuation of liberty and of equal rights to all men,
the salvation of the peopled territories of the United States
from the curse of human bondage, the prevention of the
abominable trade in men from Africa, which tends to the
Africanization and barbarization of the Continent,—these are
the stakes for which we fight.

Do you ask who is Abraham Lincoln? . . . My eyes were
never feasted with the vision of a human face, in which more
transparent honesty and more benignant kindness were combined with more of the intellect and firmness which belong
to masculine humanity. I would trust my case with the honesty and with the intellect and with the heart and with the
brain of Abraham Lincoln; and I would trust my country's
cause in the care of Abraham Lincoln as its chief magistrate,
while the wind blows and the water runs.[3]

[1] *Advertiser*, May 19, 1860; Halstead, *Caucuses of 1860*, pp. 146-150.
Andrew as chairman of his delegation was one of the committee to
inform Lincoln of his nomination.

[2] Worcester *Spy*, May 30, 1860. J. W. Baldwin was editor of the *Spy*.

[3] *Advertiser*, May 25, 1860.

In general, however, while Lincoln was praised as honest and self-made, the man to sweep the prairies,[1] many regretted the crudity of his personal appearance and his lack of polish.[2] But after the first emotion of disappointment at the sacrifice of original preferences was over, men began to open their eyes to the real excellence of the choice:—" a man full of vigorous life, rough, earnest and practical, rousing in his behalf the deepest enthusiasm among the simple people who are around him." [3] The Democrats ridiculed him as a concession to the mob, a mere local politician, known only as an adroit stump orator, " not a rail splitter but a union splitter with abolition for his wedge." [4] On the whole, however, little was said about Abraham Lincoln, for little was known.[5] Furthermore, there was little need to say anything; for this was a campaign of platforms rather than personalities.

The state convention for the nomination of governor met in Worcester, Wednesday, August 29. Governor Banks had accepted the presidency of the Illinois Central Railroad, but did not announce the fact until it was too late for it to be published in the weekly papers which went to press

---

[1] Springfield *Republican*, May 19, 26 and 31, 1860; *Advertiser*, May 19 and 21, 1860; and similarly C. R. Lowell wrote (June 30, 1860), " A man from any other section of the country would not have stood a chance in the Northwest against Douglas " (Emerson, *Life of C. R. Lowell*, p. 191).

[2] Springfield *Republican*, May 19, 1860; *Advertiser*, May 19, 1860.

[3] *Advertiser*, May 21, 1860; similarly Springfield *Republican*, May 26, 1860.

[4] *Post* quoted in the *Liberator*, June 22, 1860; *Courier*, May 19, June 2, 1860; *Post*, May 19, 1860.

[5] " Nobody knows good or bad of him."—Wendell Phillips at the New England Anti-slavery Convention, May 30, 1860, *Liberator*, June 6, 1860. There is evidence to this effect in editorials of two October *Advertisers* which defended Lincoln's probable ability to manage foreign affairs.

the Friday before the assembling of the convention.[1] He
hoped to keep local communities in ignorance of the necessity of nominating a successor and thus prevent them from
giving their delegates definite instruction, in order that in
convention they might be persuaded to vote for a conservative, preferably Henry L. Dawes. But news of the situation leaked out and Andrew's friends were instantly active.
The support of the convention was easily rallied to him,
for he had been prominent in state politics for some time
and was very popular; his recent enthusiastic report of the
Chicago convention and his appeal for the "safety and
peace of the Republic, the Union of the States, the preservation of the constitution, and the perpetuation of liberty
and equal rights to all men", had carried the people with
him. He was duly nominated.[2]

In the national Democratic convention at Charleston,
which met on April 23, we find Massachusetts men very
prominent. Caleb Cushing, of Newburyport, was its conspicuous chairman;[3] Benjamin F. Butler, of the committee
on resolutions, presented a personal minority report, which
embodied the principles and platform of 1856, demanding
popular sovereignty in the territories without reference to

[1] It was published in the New York *Tribune*, Friday, Aug. 24, and
in the Boston papers Saturday, Aug. 25.

[2] Professor Pearson, of the Institute of Technology, gives this episode in interesting detail in his *Life of Andrew*, vol. i, ch. iii. Professor Pearson treats admirably, in fact, many issues and events discussed in the present monograph, especially in the early chapters.
Parallel reference is therefore continually possible. His discussion is
naturally very personal, and so thorough is it that there is no occasion
in this work to stress or treat at length the part of Governor Andrew.

[3] The chairman of the Chicago convention was also a Massachusetts
man, George Ashmun, of Springfield, a Webster Whig in 1850. George
Ashmun, however, was less conspicuous than Caleb Cushing, and is, in
fact, remembered merely as a cool-headed moderator.

any supreme court decisions past or future.[1] The delegates, however, were not united in their support of any
policy; they disagreed, in fact, on most of the resolutions of the convention. This division of opinion was
evident on their return. Butler explained to his constituents
that it was useless to vote for Douglas, and he had therefore voted for Jefferson Davis; he said, if the Democrats
loved Douglas more than their party, then he had failed to
do his duty as a delegate, but if they loved their party they
would not condemn him.[2] Of the other faction, Isaac
Davis explained to his constituents in Worcester:

We were willing to stand upon all the provisions of the Constitution, as expounded by the Supreme Court; but when they
asked us to go one step further, and ignore popular sovereignty, and deny the right of man to self-government, and
make slavery a national institution, for myself I could not and
would not consent.[3]

This same division of opinion persisted in Baltimore
where, because of the failure of the Charleston convention
to make nominations, the delegates reassembled on June 18.
Here, as at Charleston, Caleb Cushing was elected chairman; but here he resigned because he did not approve of
the exclusion of the Charleston seceders. On the call of
the states, he with fifteen other Massachusetts delegates led
by Benjamin F. Butler, withdrew from the convention.
While those remaining voted for Douglas, the sixteen

---

[1] E. D. Fite, *Campaign of 1860*, p. 106; Halstead, *Caucuses of 1860*,
pp. 46-56.

[2] *Post*, May 17, 1860. Speech of Butler at Lowell, May 15, 1860.

[3] Worcester *Spy*, May 14, 1860. "There is a crack in the democratic
party, and there is a nigger in the crack, and the nigger cannot be got
out of it," was the caustic comment of the Springfield *Republican*, June
22, 1860. Less caustically, the Worcester *Spy*, April 30, 1860.

seceders with one hundred sixty-seven or more from other states met in convention which, with Caleb Cushing presiding, adopted the majority report of Charleston and nominated Breckinridge and Lane.[1]

Early in the campaign Douglas visited Massachusetts. Crowds gathered to hear him. Warrington[2] declared that "the mobs" went to hear the man who had destroyed the hitherto invincible Democratic party.[3] But although he could win applause for his views of popular sovereign from even an anti-slavery audience,[4] he did not unite the Democrats of Massachusetts.

Two separate nominating conventions met September 12: the Douglas men in Springfield, the nationals in Boston. The Springfield meeting, with Oliver Stevens as chairman, adopted resolutions which, adhering to the Democratic doctrine of 1848 and 1856, opposed the exercise of any jurisdiction by Congress over the matter of slavery in the territories,[5] and nominated Erasmus Beach for governor.[6] The meeting in Tremont Temple, Boston, was a more enthusiastic gathering. Here the seceders of Baltimore were conspicuous: Dr. George B. Loring presided, Benjamin F. Butler was nominated for governor and Caleb Cushing made an important speech. In general, the speeches condemned the democracy of squatter sovereignty, and stood for the democracy which had proclaimed: " It is the

---

[1] *Advertiser*, June 14 to 25, 1860; Halstead, *op. cit.*, pp. 205-206, 224.

[2] W. S. Robinson, the Boston correspondent of the Springfield *Republican*. *Cf.* appendix ii, p. 204 and note 3; and Pearson, *op. cit.*, vol. i, p. 59.

[3] Springfield *Republican*, July 20, 1860.

[4] Springfield *Republican*, July 21, 1860.

[5] *Post*, Sept. 13, 1860.

[6] Erasmus Beach had been the Democratic nominee every year since 1855.

duty of the Federal Government, in all its departments, to protect, when necessary, the rights of persons and property in the Territories and wherever else its constitutional authority extends." But Caleb Cushing attacked the Republican party, declaring that its motive power, its mainspring, its vital spirit, was anti-slavery fanaticism. He denounced John A. Andrew for defending the Personal-Liberty Laws. He asserted the alleged belief of the Southern Democrats that if Mr. Lincoln should be elected, the Republicans would be obliged, under penalty of prompt dissolution, to attack the domestic rights of the states. Moreover, he held that Southerners would be unworthy the name of Americans if they did not defend their rights by constitutional means, and if necessary by extra-constitutional means. Therefore he concluded: " Let all those among us who, in the blind zeal of stupid negro worship, would thus drive the Southern states into revolution, go on."

Yet notwithstanding such threats of danger, and the confidence of prominent leaders that salvation lay in the election of Breckinridge, and notwithstanding the loyal support of the Boston *Post*, which in March, 1860, had said, " Seward's irrepressible conflict can bring no good to our New England manufactures. *Vote it down!*",[1] still when the election came, Breckinridge polled but a small

---

[1] The *Post* had quarreled with Douglas on Kansas issues and opposed him consistently, and (June 25, 1860) it blamed him for the split in the party; (on May 2, 1860 an editorial demanded conciliation on terms of the supreme court decision) and on May 19 it asked: " Will the vast commercial manufacturing interests of the North indorse this horrible and suicidal war on the South?" In line with this question, Fite, *op. cit.*, p. 121, says: " The merchant class of the North East became conspicuously lukewarm for Seward after the cry for John Brown began to threaten the loss of Southern trade."

part of the total vote, and was beaten by Douglas in every
county save Barnstable and Nantucket.[1]

A so-called Third party had been organized in Boston,
on December 8, 1859. " In view of the present disturbed
condition of public sentiment and dangers which threaten
our union ", a call had been sent to those " who honor and
cherish that Union—who mean to maintain the constitution
of the United States, and faithfully to carry out all its requirements and obligations." They met[2] soon after the
John Brown episode, and the speeches of Edward Everett
and Caleb Cushing discussed that outrage. Resolutions
were adopted sympathizing with the people of Virginia,

[1] Vote by counties in 1860:

COUNTIES.	REPUBLICAN.		DOUGLAS DEM.		BRECKINRIDGE DEM.		UNION.	
	Pres.	Gov.	Pres.	Gov.	Pres.	Gov.	Pres.	Gov.
Essex	14,805	14,583	4,277	4,318	889	821	3,188	3,313
Middlesex.	17,580	16,954	7,022	6,878	923	847	4,794	4,975
Suffolk ...	10,306	9,906	4,783	4,795	937	1,041	5,426	5,708
Norfolk ..	8,864	8,628	3,590	3,552	452	425	2,987	3,149
Plymouth .	6,855	6,795	1,432	1,421	284	278	1,874	1,907
Barnstable.	2,367	2,341	134	134	408	421	343	359
Bristol ...	7,854	7,460	1,752	1,673	465	361	673	635
Worcester	16,015	15,722	4,862	4,696	302	283	1,744	1,893
Franklin ...	4,051	3,895	914	879	328	341	135	148
Hampshire.	5,184	5,081	1,742	2,094	522	585	299	315
Hampden .	4,598	4,552	578	624	229	234	182	198
Berkshire .	5,209	5,123	2,782	2,877	199	124	238	351
Dukes	342	342	155	121	64	58	58	52
Nantucket.	437	420	32	32	69	71	76	76

These figures are taken from the *Advertiser*. They vary a trifle from
those in the *Tribune Almanac*, but, inasmuch as the almanac did not
give the votes for governor, and since the purpose is comparison, it
seemed wise to take both from the same source.

[2] Levi Lincoln was president; six of the vice-presidents were George
Peabody, George Ticknor Curtis, Benjamin E. Bates, Luther V. Bell,
Benjamin F. Butler and Amos A. Lawrence. These men continued to
be prominent in affairs and illustrate types of opinion.

and lamenting intestine dissensions. The assembled delegates, furthermore, declared unchangeable union indispensable to the prosperity of all and to our existence as a civilized nation, and proposed zealously to cultivate and promote every influence likely to advance and maintain the
most amicable relations among the whole people of the
United States.[1]

Those who joined the party were conservatives, mainly
Cotton Whigs, who believed with Rufus Choate that
" Union of the states " stood above everything else, and
that slavery and other evils would come to an end sooner if
the Union should be preserved than if any division should
be made.[2]   The party therefore became a league on the
Union platform against Democrats, North and South.[3]   It
was opposed to the Republicans also, because of the presence among them of abolitionists, said by George Hillard

[1] Merriam (*Life of Bowles*, vol. i, p. 264) says: " This party recognized what the *Republican* and its party wholly failed to appreciate—
that the union was in imminent danger." In substantiation of this is a
manuscript letter from Edward Everett to Robert C. Winthrop, Nov.
13, 1859: " It [the Harper's Ferry affair] is a natural result of the
anti-slavery agitation. That has been for years carried on; and is one
of the Precursors of the final catastrophe, which cannot, I think, be
far distant."

[2] From a letter of the late Rufus Choate, nephew of the great orator;
also S. G. Brown, *Life of Choate*, p. 303, " We join ourselves to no
party that does not carry the flag and keep step to the music of the
union "; and *cf.* introduction, *supra*, p. 16. Similarly the *Courier*, May
26, 1860.

[3] A letter from Amos A. Lawrence to J. J. Crittenden, of Kentucky,
Jan. 6, 1860, shows that Lawrence was a prime mover. He wrote: " If
you will send me two notes of three lines each in your own handwrit-
ing, asking me whether the Union-loving men of Massachusetts are
ready to unite with the opponents of the democratic party in the other
states for the defeat of that party and all extremists, I will promise to
organize this whole state in eight weeks."

to be the life-blood and vital force of the Republican party.[1]
But exactly what policy would be pursued on definite issues
by the new organization was unknown; all that was clear
was that its members believed agitation injurious to the
welfare of the country and that the platform of the Republicans was unwise.[2] They even prophesied in September,
1860, that in the event of Lincoln's election a Southern
convention would consult on advising congressmen from
the Southern states to resign.[3] Furthermore, they believed
their candidates (Bell and Everett, nominated in Baltimore) to be better qualified by both education and experience than were the candidates of the Republican party.[4]

So much for the theories of the new party. Statistics
show some interesting facts. First, some of its members
believed that although Bell was high-minded and honorable,
his was a statesmanship of the past. This faction (smaller
by statistics than by reputation) voted for Lincoln.[5] Second, the vote throughout the state shows that the Union
party was of Boston and its environs; its only appreciable
strength was in the eastern counties where were the trading
centers — Essex, Middlesex, Suffolk and Norfolk. Plymouth and Worcester had a few more than the other agri-

[1] *Courier*, Mar. 30, 1860. Hillard's speech at the convention, Mar. 29,
1860. George Hillard with George Lunt edited the Boston *Courier*.

[2] *Advertiser* and Springfield *Republican*, March 30, 1860; Merriam,
op. cit., vol. i, p. 263. The drafts of resolutions made by George Hillard, George T. Curtis and Amos A. Lawrence, found among the *Lawrence MSS*, substantiate this statement.

[3] *Courier*, Sept. 8, 1860. Report of a Constitutional Union meeting.

[4] *Courier*, May 11, and June 27, 1860.

[5] Dr. Samuel A. Green (late vice-president of the Massachusetts Historical Society) said this was true in his own case and true also in
that of many of his friends. With the exception of Berkshire, Hampden, Bristol and the islands, the Union vote for governor was larger
than for president.

cultural counties.[1] This statistical fact substantiates Henry L. Dawes' characterization of the party as "a class of simple-minded people who believe that the sun rises in Chelsea, comes up over State Street, hovers about the state house, and sinks in the waters of Back Bay."[2] They were the elderly Whigs "who turned their eyes from the future back to the past" and refused to be gathered into the Republican party, who objected to John A. Andrew's Brownism though they forgot that their candidate for governor, Amos A. Lawrence, had been chairman of the Kansas Emigrant Aid Committee. And, third, election returns show that the only success achieved by the Union Party was the election of Appleton instead of Burlingame as Congressman in the fifth district.[3]

Another local episode of the campaign was the contest between Goldsmith F. Bailey, nominee of the Republican party for the ninth district, and Eli Thayer, its former representative. The regular Republican organization rejected Thayer because his vote on the New Mexico bill showed his absolute belief in popular sovereignty.[4] They

---

[1] *Cf. supra*, p. 33, note 1.

[2] *Advertiser,* Sept. 19, 1860. Sumner characterized the same party as "Brahmins who imagine themselves of better clay than others, or of Chinese themselves, cousins of the Sun and Moon."—*Works*, vol. v, p. 343. And his friend Edward L. Pierce called them "antipathetic to the anti-slavery sentiments," and claimed that the five thousand votes given to Bell and Everett were cast by those having "a mercantile interest or connection."—Pierce, *Life of Sumner*, vol. iii, p. 619.

[3] William Appleton had been elected to Congress for 1851-1855 against Burlingame, nominee of the Free-Soilers. He was a wealthy manufacturer of high character.—Adams, *Life of Dana*, vol. ii, p. 248. He resigned in 1861 and was succeeded by Samuel Hooper.

[4] Worcester *Spy*, June 4 and Aug. 4, 1860.—He did not vote to remove slavery from New Mexico, for he said Congress could not pass territorial bills. Sumner argued against Thayer: "Let it be the Popular Sovereignty of the American people, counted by millions and assembled in congress, rather than the tyrannical irresponsible sovereignty of a handful of squatters."—*Works*, vol. v, p. 335.

claimed that he was more Democratic than the Democrats, even though he was an active anti-slavery man. All the newspapers opposed him, so that his support, aside from his own speeches, was through broadsides published by an organization friendly to him, the Central Republican Club,[1] which was not a part of the regular Republican organization. These broadsides went to prove that Thayer, as a delegate to the national convention, supported the Chicago platform. But when he desired a public debate with Sumner, the accepted Republican, Thayer put himself in opposition to the organized party, who claimed that he was in league with the Democrats.[2] Thus although his own efforts won him many votes, yet his own popularity could not offset party influence,[3] and Goldsmith F. Bailey was elected.

Aside from these two episodes in the fifth and ninth districts, there seems to have been little interest in the candidates. Occasionally, in the eastern part of the state, Wide-Awakes, each uniformed in cap and cape, and carrying a lamp on a staff, paraded through the streets and aroused a momentary enthusiasm.[4] But in 1860 there was no one burning question such as " bleeding Kansas " of

[1] A few of these broadsides are in the possession of Miss Eva Thayer.

[2] *Sumner MSS*, Thayer to Sumner, Oct. 29, 1860, and Baldwin to Sumner, Oct. 29, 1860.

[3] The vote of Worcester county for congressman — Bailey 9,776, Thayer 7,953, scattering 134.—*Spy*, Nov. 8, 1860. Hoar, in his *Autobiography*, vol. i, p. 190, makes the following characterization: "Thayer was a sincere anti-slavery man. But he liked to do things in peculiar and original ways of his own, and was impatient of slow and old-fashioned methods. So he got estranged from his Republican brethren, and, defeated in 1860, took no part in public activities during the war, became somewhat soured, and landed in the Democratic party."

[4] Sumner, *Works*, vol. v, p. 344, note. The Bangor Wide-Awakes came to Boston for a demonstration. They were headed by eight giants, and six Penobscot Indians in war costume. There were ten thousand Wide-Awakes present. Also Worcester *Spy*, Oct. 18, 1860.

1856. Instead the platform dealt with a general policy, and few except leaders and thinkers were conscious of a crisis.[1] Indeed the vote, which maintained a substantial Republican majority had not increased over that of four years previous.[2] Yet notwithstanding these facts and figures the opposition was not inconsiderable; it was persistent, insistent and strong out of proportion to its numbers. Nevertheless when the election was over, the customary acquiescence prevailed. The Constitutional Unionists, in particular, were willing to wait and see how things would turn out; they were willing to allow the Republicans a fair chance. They professed to see the advantage of Lincoln's being a western man, for he would not need to make New England fanaticism, or New York political anti-slavery, a part of his politics; they therefore advised the South to pause and see what manner of man had been elected, for he, as president-elect, was entitled to the forbearance and consideration due the representative of the people. Accordingly the *Courier* declared: " The government of the United States *is* a government " which " must obey the law of its being, in whosesoever hands its authority is lodged." [3] Of the minority, a few extreme radicals, always demanding abolition even at the cost of union, could not be satisfied by a Republican victory, but the most conceded with Wendell Phillips that the election of Lincoln was a milestone marking progress; for, although he did not claim

---

[1] Lowell, *Atlantic* (October, 1860), vol. vi, p. 492; Merriam, *op. cit.*, vol. i, p. 259; Springfield *Republican*, Aug. 6, 1860. C. F. Adams, *Autobiography* (p. 69), claims that his father, even, and Sumner had no conception of the momentousness of the crisis.

[2]	Rep.	Dem.	Fillmore-Am.	Consti.-Union
1856	108,190	39,240	19,626	
1860	106,533	34,372 (Douglas)		22,331
		5,939 (Breckinridge)		

[3] *Courier*, Nov. 10 and 17, 1860.

that the negro should be a citizen, still the president-elect represented an anti-slavery idea.[1]   And since this was true, a number of pronounced Democrats persistently prophesied disaster, for, believing that safety to the Union lay in non-interference by Congress with slavery in any state or territory, they held that the " rail-splitter " would become the " union-splitter." [2]   Nevertheless, in spite of all the threats and prophecies of disunion preceding and following the election, the victors, believing that these threats were used merely for political intimidation,[3] were confident, now that the election was over, that things would quiet down.   Following the Republican triumph, then, victors and vanquished united in a common feeling of confidence and security.

[1] Sears, *Wendell Phillips*, p. 212.

[2] *Liberator*, June 22, 1860, quoted from the *Post*. The *Pilot* was less rabid than the *Post*. It said it would not do anything for or against those elected. And it even hoped that by March 4 the passions of the campaign should have subsided.—Nov. 17, 1860. But on March 2, 1861, the *Post* declared: " We are the political opponents of the Republican party, and expect to remain so."

[3] *Advertiser*, Sept. 11, 1860; Worcester *Spy*, Oct. 25, 1860; *Bee*, Nov. 2, 1860; Hampshire *Gazette*, Nov. 13, 1860; Springfield *Republican*, Nov. 10, 1860, said: " The South understands its interests too well to be betrayed into such a mistake." Sumner at Framingham, October 11, showed that seven times since the adoption of the constitution the menace of disunion had been made to play its part, and there was nothing in it which should not be treated with indignant contempt, as it was merely a threat and nothing more.—*Works*, vol. v, pp. 296-300.

CHAPTER II

The Period of the Secessions—November 7 to April 15, 1860 [1]

Active measures of disunion on the part of South Carolina soon disturbed, even within Republican circles, the feeling of confidence which prevailed after the election. Indeed, real serious action came as a surprise, for, although there had been much talk about secession before the election, the belief that it was a mere threat had been widespread and confidently held, and there seemed for a time to be indifference as to the portentousness of events. The New York *Tribune*, for example, conceded that the South was right,[2] and the Springfield *Republican* said that the universal expression of all parties was: "If South Carolina wants to go out of the Union, let her go and say no more about it." [3] Apathy to disunion was, in fact, so great that

[1] There is no election within these months whereby we may ascertain in figures the numbers of adherents to various opinions. It is a period of discussion merely. Newspapers, pamphlets, memoirs, and correspondence—published and unpublished—are abundant. It is from this mass of material that the chapter has been compiled. Its purpose is to show the gradations of opinion from the union-breaking abolitionist to the pro-slavery conciliator.

[2] November 30, 1860.

[3] November 16, 1860. In the same tenor Washington Gladden tells that Henry Ward Beecher, in Boston, replied to the question, Will they secede? with, "I don't believe they will, and I don't care if they do." *Recollections* p. 102. And among the *Sumner MSS* a letter from Edward Everett Hale is dated: "December 21, 1860, and of the Disunited States the first day." Moreover, he remarked: "We are taking

an agent of the Southern states found no difficulty in purchasing arms and ammunition in the neighborhood of Springfield.[1] Furthermore, the " reliable " *Advertiser*, whose standard was the stock market, said there was no great cause for alarm; it argued that the South could not persist in a policy which would bring commercial distress to her communities.[2]

Nevertheless, as early as November 10, the same paper had remarked that an uneasy feeling was arising among Northern capitalists, which is evidence that the South Carolina movement was beginning to be taken seriously. A little later the *Advertiser* asserted that secession had no validity under the Constitution,[3] and on December 22, that South Carolina was as much in the union as ever.[4] Thus when vague threat became reality all indifference vanished. It was all wrong, unconstitutional and unwarrantable, was the verdict of the anti-Republican *Courier*,[5] which, in the bitterness of the campaign, had prophesied that Republican victory would " carry disunion with it as a logical result." [6]

secession with due calmness here." Even Sumner himself, C. F. Adams, Jr., came to believe, was also of this opinion when opposing Adams and conciliatory measures in the winter of 1861. *Autobiography*, p. 86.

[1] The Springfield *Republican*, December 29, 1860, attributed the indifference not to any disloyalty, but to the fact that the people had heard the cry so often that they paid no attention to it.

[2] November 12 and 15, 1860. Also the view of the Worcester *Spy*, November 14, 1860; and the *Liberator*, November 16, 1860, asked: " Will they secede from the Union? Will they jump into the Atlantic? Will they conflagrate their own dwellings, cut their own throats, and enable their slaves to rise in successful insurrection? Perhaps they will—probably they will not! By their bullying and raving they have many times frightened the North into a base submission to their demands—they expect to do it again!"

[3] *Advertiser*, Nov. 16, 1860.

[4] Also the view of the Springfield *Republican*, Dec. 25, 1860.

[5] *Courier*, Nov. 26, 1860.   [6] *Courier*, Aug. 1, 1860.

John Bell, presidential candidate of the Constitutional Unionists, expressed the party's position, saying: "By no principle of public law, by no code of morals, by no law of earth or heaven, would Mississippi or any other state be justified, under existing circumstances, in withdrawing from the Union.[1] Even the Breckinridge *Post*, by March, declared: "Secession can be justified upon no basis whatever.   It is utterly wrong." [2]

In fact, in January, when Amos A. Lawrence described the general sentiment, he could write:

It turns out that the nullifiers have no party, not a solitary press, nor so far as can be seen a single sympathizer in any of the non-slaveholding States.   On the contrary their violence has welded together the whole Northern people in one compact body, determined to sustain the Government at Washington—the Democrats of both wings are equally decided with the Republicans.[3]

These defenders of the union defined it as "a government of the people instituted by the people of all the states," [4] not a compact between the states which any states may rescind at pleasure.[5]   Secession, consequently, was declared

[1] *Advertiser*, Dec. 13, 1860.   [2] *Post*, March 2, 1861.

[3] *Lawrence MSS*, to S. R. Sneed, Jan. 15, 1861.

[4] *Advertiser*, Jan. 23, 1861.   The Worcester *Spy*, Dec. 4, 1860, said: "The people of the states created this compact, and they alone can destroy it."   Gov. Banks declared that "Whether the government is a compact between states or a union of the people, it is nevertheless a government, and cannot be dissolved at the bidding of any dissatisfied party." *Mass. Senate Doc.*, 1861, no. i, p. 35.

[5] Parker, in "The Right of Secession," published in *North American Review*, vol. xciii, p. 224, said: "It is a perversion of terms to call the 'supreme law of the land' a compact between the states, which any state may rescind at pleasure.   It is not itself an agreement, but is the result of an agreement."   Similarly, J. F. Clarke, *Secession* (pam.), pp. 21, 22.

to have no legal meaning, for the Constitution of the United States acts directly upon the citizens and not through the state upon them. Moreover, the Constitution and the laws of the United States were held to be " the supreme law; and the act of a state, ordinance or statute, which conflicts with that supreme law, shrivels into a nullity. To attempt to defeat it by a resolution is folly. To attempt to defeat the National Government by organized resistance, by force of arms, is treason." [1]

In this connection Lowell, the most politically wise of the literary men, explained clearly that " the United States are not a German Confederation, but a unitary and indivisible nation, with a national life to protect, a national power to maintain, and national rights to defend against any and every assailant, at all hazards." In the same connection he humorously suggests that if secession is a right, each state may exercise such a right at any time it sees fit, and " we shall need something like a Fugitive Law for runaway republics," and we must secure treaty provisions that foreign powers " shall help us catch any delinquent who may take refuge with them." [2] Therefore it seemed to him, as to many others, that the nation needed an Andrew Jackson, " an hour of Old Hickory, or old Rough-and-Ready—some man who could take command and crystalize this chaos into order." [3]

There were some, however, who differed from this opinion. Caleb Cushing, for example, said to the citizens of Newburyport: " If the people cannot overcome the Republicans and compel them to cease from agitation of the

---

[1] Thomas, *Suggestions upon the Personal-Liberty Law and " Secession" (so-called)*, (pam.) p. 17.

[2] *Atlantic Monthly* (Feb., 1861), vol. vii, p. 237, " E Pluribus Unum."

[3] Lowell, *Letters*, vol. i, p. 308. Similarly, Springfield *Republican*, Dec. 17, 1860, and Worcester *Spy*, Dec. 22, 1860.

slavery question, it may be best to separate; best for us at the North as for them at the South." [1]   Likewise Robert C. Winthrop regarded the Southern people as fully entitled to achieve their independence if they saw fit, although he doubted that it would be to their advantage.[2]   And Edward Everett, not yet joined to the party of the Union, said: "If our sister states must leave us, in the name of heaven let them go in peace." [3]

The Abolitionists as well as the pro-slavery sympathizers would let them go; both were, in fact, glad of the secession movement.   Indeed these reformers rejoiced over the thought of a Northern confederacy, freed from responsibility for the protection of a system of bondage; the diseased section would be "sloughed off".   They would not now have to withdraw from the Union,[4] for without the slave states the Constitution was no longer "a Covenant with Death and an Agreement with Hell";[5] they could, therefore, share in the government with a clear conscience. Their jubilation was boldly voiced by Wendell Phillips in Boston on January 20, when he said:

"The Lord reigneth; let the earth rejoice," . . . "the Covenant with Death" is annulled. . . . "The Agreement with Hell" is broken in pieces.   The chain which has held the slave system since 1787 is parted.   Thirty years ago Southern

[1] *Post*, Dec. 13, 1860.   Speech of Caleb Cushing.

[2] Winthrop, *Memoirs*, p. 219.

[3] Letter from Edward Everett in the *Post*, Feb. 6, 1861.

[4] *Liberator*, July 6, 1861; Sears, *Wendell Phillips*, pp. 217-218.   Later they condemned the action of the South because it was unjustifiable, while their own demands were for the principles of the Declaration of Independence; *Liberator*, April 19, 1861.

[5] The motto of the *Liberator* in 1861 was: "The Constitution is a Covenant with Death and an Agreement with Hell."   Later, on December 13, 1861, it was changed to, "Proclaim Liberty throughout the Land to all the Inhabitants thereof."

leaders, sixteen years ago Northern Abolitionists, announced their purpose to seek the dissolution of the American union. Who dreamed that success would come so soon![1]

Neither of these groups, the pro-slavery sympathizers and the Abolitionists, would, of course, make any effort to reunite the states; nor would they approve of any compromise.[2] Furthermore, Abolitionists were opposed to war as such; and, according to this ideal, their *Liberator* demanded: " LET THERE BE NO CIVIL WAR, but A SEPARATION BETWEEN THE FREE AND SLAVE STATES, IN THE SPIRIT OF ABRAHAM AND LOT." The Quakers naturally joined in this peace policy.[3] And even some anti-slavery men who were not extreme Abolitionists thought the national partnership by no means worth restoring; they had " a horror

[1] Reported in the *Liberator*, January 25, 1861. Similar sentiment is found in *Sumner MSS*, in letters from William L. Garrison (February 25, 1861), from Albert G. Browne (December 19, 1860), from Amasa Walker (April 13, 1861), from William Claflin (January 4, 1861), and from F. W. Bird (January 6, 1861). Also in pamphlets, Blanchard, *The War of Secession*, and J. F. Clarke, *Secession*. The latter said: " We must not sacrifice the soul of our institutions for the sake of preserving the body; for we should, in that case, have only a dead body."

[2] Phillips: " You may as well dam up Niagara with bulrushes as bind our anti-slavery purpose with Congressional Compromise."—*Liberator*, January 25, 1861. And Amasa Walker (in *Sumner MSS*, April 13, 1861) : " I think we ought to do all we can to get them out as soon as possible."

[3] Whittier wrote, " 16, 1 mo., 1861," *A Word for the Hour:*—

> " They break the links of Union, shall we light
> The fires of Hell to weld anew the chain
> On that red anvil where each blow is pain?
>
> *   *   *   *   *   *   *   *
>
> Pity, forgive, but urge them back no more."

Whittier also wrote Sumner, March 31, 1861: " The conflicting rumors of Washington trouble me. I am for peace, not by conceding our principles, but by simply telling the slave states to ' go '—border ones and all." Pierce, *Life of Sumner*, vol. iv, p. 5.

of war and grave doubt whether such a question could be settled by force." Indeed, for a time it seemed more than doubtful whether the Northern people had any strong and passionate sentiment of love for the Union, such as would inspire them to fight for its maintenance.[1]

On the whole, in the North there were, as Merriam says, two general sentiments: first, " the government must not give up its own to the seceders, must not surrender its forts or renounce the collection of customs duties "; second, " it was impracticable to compel by arms the submission and return of the seceded states," [2] for, as the judicious *Republican* said, " The United States are infinitely better off without them than with them, if only chained to the Union by force and fear." But, although that paper advocated a peace policy, it believed there was a point beyond which forbearance was submission;[3] and that precise point was clear to all minds: when a state or any portion of its people resist the laws, the government must enforce them. This brings us back to the first proposition of Merriam that the government must not give up its own to the seceders, must not renounce the collection of customs duties.[4]

[1] Merriam, *Life of Bowles*, vol. i, p. 284; also Springfield *Republican*, November 2, 1860; and Gladden, *Recollections*, p. 103, says: "Up to the middle of December this policy was tentatively advocated by a good many anti-slavery men. The reason for it was in the horror of war, and in the grave doubt whether such a question could be settled by force. Gradually these doubts were overborne, and the Websterian sentiment of the indissolubility of the union began to prevail."

[2] Merriam, *op. cit.*, vol. i, p. 283. And *Advertiser*, Nov. 16, 1860: "There will be no holding of the state as a conquered province; it will simply be a case of the paralysis of the arm of federal authority within the state."

[3] Springfield *Republican*, March 19, 1861.

[4] Hampshire *Gazette*, Dec. 4, 1860; Springfield *Republican*, Dec. 25, 1860; *Advertiser*, Dec. 28, 1860; Thomas, *Suggestions upon the Personal-Liberty Law and Secession (so-called)*, (pam.) p. 20.

The various gradations of opinion are well described by Oliver Wendell Holmes in a letter to John Lothrop Motley, February 16, 1861 :

From the impracticable Abolitionist, as bent on total separation from the South as Carolina is on secession from the North, to the Hunker, or Submissionist, or whatever you chose to call the wretch who would sacrifice every thing and beg the South's pardon for offending it, you find all shades of opinion in our streets. If Mr. Seward or Mr. Adams moves in favor of compromise, the whole Republican party sways, like a field of grain, before the breath of either of them. If Mr. Lincoln says he shall execute the laws and collect the revenue, though the heavens cave in, the backs of the Republicans stiffen again, and they take down the old Revolutionary king's arms, and begin to ask whether they can be altered to carry minié bullets.[1]

The " Hunker or Submissionist " referred to was largely of the manufacturing and trading interests. Of such John Murray Forbes wrote to Sumner : "Our money people here have been badly frightened and many decent-looking men, if called upon to act now, would try to have a kind of compromise made that would promise to patch up difficulties and their pockets." [2]   Repeated evidence of this financial embarrassment may be found in contemporary correspondence; Charles Eliot Norton, for example, wrote : " There is universal alarm, general financial pressure, great commercial embarrassment. The course of trade between the North and the South is interrupted, many manufacturing establishments are closed or working on short time, and there are many failures; and many workmen thrown out of employment." [3]   And from North Bridgewater, Ply-

---

[1] Morse, *Life and Letters of Holmes*, vol. ii, p. 154.

[2] *Sumner MSS*, from John Murray Forbes, December 22, 1860.

[3] C. E. Norton, *Letters*, vol. i, p. 213, to A. H. Clough, December, 1860.

mouth County, Sumner learned that many people " are suffering extremely from the general depression of Business. A large number of our Manufacturers, who depend wholly upon Southern Trade, are unable to continue business, thus throwing hundreds of our poor Mechanics out of employment." [1]

The individual case of a Harvard student is of interest in this connection; he wrote to President Felton:

When I first entered College, last September, I fully expected to be able to pay the charge of advanced standing amounting to ($45) forty-five Dollars. But my father, who is connected with the Southern trade, has experienced many difficulties in meeting his payments and requests me to petition the Corporation of Harvard College to defer the payment of the charge until next term. [2]

In the interests of this class the Reverend J. J. Bowen, rector of St. Stephen's, Pittsfield, made a plea for conciliation; [3] he explained how credit had been shaken already, and concluded:

If then this union be actually severed, would not public and private credit be instantly destroyed, commerce suspended, and an arrest put upon every industry? How long would the manufacturers of Pittsfield and New England, wealthy as

[1] *Sumner MSS*, from L. B. Holbrook, December 22, 1860.

[2] *Harvard College Papers*, Second Series, vol. xxviii (1861), from W. M. Howland, March 4, 1861.

[3] It would be interesting to know how many conservative and Constitutional Union men belonged to the Protestant Episcopal Church. Amos A. Lawrence and his family connections, the Appletons and Dr. Samuel A. Green were Episcopalians, as were Robert C. Winthrop and George Ticknor. These names are not proof but merely suggestive as evidence of the assertion sometimes made that the conservatives in 1860 were of the same social and financial position as the Tories of the Revolution.

they are, be able to furnish employment? I firmly believe
that in 90 days the doors of every mill would be closed. . . .
No words of mine can portray the distress, the poverty, the
crime and the despair.[1]

And when in February there was a shoemakers' strike in
Lynn, Haverhill and Marblehead, the *Post,* the New York
Herald, Democrats, manufacturers and strikers blamed the
anti-slavery agitation. They argued that the South was
boycotting the shoes; that with the consequent decrease in
business wages had been lowered, with the result of the
strike.[2]

Meanwhile the compromise policies which Holmes said
swayed the Republicans were being advocated by Seward
in the Senate and Adams in the House. On January 31, in
his speech *On the State of the Union,* Adams conceded to

[1] *Courier,* Dec. 16, 1860.

[2] *Post,* Feb. 21 and Mar. 9, 1860. On February 24 a letter from a
Boston merchant to an acquaintance in Concord, N. H., was published.
It stated that the actual fluctuations of trade were probably to some
extent the cause of the strike; but that the great cause was something
else. " Our great market the South," it explained, " is for the present
nearly lost to us. Our former large customers there now either de-
cline to make any purchases, or buy very sparingly. The reason is, the
state of feeling there, caused by recent events, toward the North. This
agitation of the slavery question may be sport or profit to politicians,
but I fear that unless it cease, so as to allow a change of feeling there
soon, it will be death to us so far as our trade is concerned."

Carroll D. Wright, however, in *Strikes in Massachusetts 1830-1880,*
shows that there had been strikes nearly every year. Yet this particular
one was very widespread. A big demonstration was planned for February 22; disturbances continued to occur until April. An overstocked
market and an influx of farmers, masons, carpenters into shoemaking
during winter months lowered the price of labor. Therefore the statement that slack southern trade was entirely responsible may be questioned. Nevertheless, the fact that the trade was slack made good
political capital, and the use of that fact is one incident in which mercantile interest shows itself openly condemning anti-slavery agitation
and demanding remedy.

the South all the territory belonging to the United States
in which slaves could be made useful, and was willing that
slave-owners should have means of recovering runaway
slaves in the spirit of the Constitution. He moreover ridiculed South Carolina and Georgia for apprehending possible infringement upon their rights, because, he asserted,
no law could be availing which was contrary to the sympathies of the people.[1] Such concessions pleased the anti-
Republican press;[2] and in order to strengthen the support
of such conciliatory statesmanship a Union meeting was
held in Faneuil Hall on February 5.[3] The enthusiasm for
this amicable policy was so great that Amos A. Lawrence
wrote his wife that he feared the slave states must go; for
the peace party was strengthening, and the Republicans
would have an enemy at home to contend with.[4] The Republican press itself divided on the issue; the *Tribune* called
it "mistaken magnanimity"[5] some preferred separation
to such concessions, others approved. The Abolitionists,
naturally, ridiculed the policy as "capping Vesuvius with a
sheet of straw paper."[6] It is thus evident that the purpose
of Adams was not widely understood, for dissatisfaction
and distrust existed even though his support was general.
There was, of course, no opportunity for any public expla-

[1] *Cong. Globe*, 36 cong., 2 sess., app., pp. 126-127.

[2] *Courier*, Feb. 2, 1861; *Sumner MSS*, from J. M. Forbes, Jan. 16,
1861.

[3] *Post*, Feb. 6, 1861; *Courier*, Feb. 6, 1861.

[4] *Lawrence MSS*, to Mrs. Lawrence, Feb. 10, 1861.

[5] Feb. 26, 1861; also *Sumner MSS*, from F. W. Bird, Jan. 6, and from
B. Coolidge, Jan. 18, 1861 (who even classed Adams with Benedict
Arnold), and from William Claflin, president of the Massachusetts
senate, Jan. 4, 1861.

[6] *Liberator*, Jan. 18, 1861.

nation, nor was it like Adams to try to explain [1] that his purpose was to keep the representatives occupied in this discussion to bridge the interval before March 4 in peace and quiet.[2]   But, fortunately for him, there was a sufficient number who perceived the intent to make it possible for him and his colleagues to persist in delay.[3]

Within the state those favoring conciliation worked for three things: the Crittenden compromise, the Virginia Peace Conference, and the repeal of the Personal Liberty Law.   And those stressful days of compromise continued from the Union meeting in Faneuil Hall, on February 5, until the modification of the Personal Liberty Law, on March 25.   The initial demonstration, for Union through compromise, adopted resolutions favoring the Crittenden propositions, and appointed a committee of " union savers "

[1] Adams to Andrew, Feb. 8, 1861: " I presume that you have known me long enough to believe that neither praise nor blame has much effect in regulating my public action—My duty is performed."

[2] What that purpose was has been explained from time to time, for example: Massachusetts Historical Society, *Proceedings*, Dec. 1911, p. 246; Adams, *Life of Adams*, pp. 130-134; Adams, *Life of Dana*, vol. ii, p. 253; Schouler, *History of Massachusetts*, vol. i, p. 5. But the most satisfactory statement is in the recent *Autobiography* of C. F. Adams, p. 73.

[3] *Sumner MSS*, Jan. 18, 1861. Charles E. Norton wrote Sumner that Longfellow, Lowell and George W. Curtis were satisfied and believed in the policy to gain time. He also said: " No one here is for compromise."   Similarly Boutwell, *Reminiscences*, vol. i, p. 271. Adams was, however, so little understood that he was not received by the people of substantial position until after his return from his post in England, when his eminent services demanded recognition. Even then Sumner did not forgive him for his position in 1861, which broke the friendship between Adams and Sumner. And in consequence the Sumner faction did not welcome the distinguished minister on his return. This is evident from a letter of Edward L. Pierce to Sumner on July 24, 1868; he wrote: " The Adams reception has taken place. Of course I did not go. Few men who are active and of account were there. The hall was only half full."—(*Sumner MSS*)

to take their resolutions to Washington.[1]   Within the next few days petitions were widely circulated and won many signatures, with the result that on February 12 Crittenden presented to the Senate a petition favoring his measures signed by 22,313 citizens of Massachusetts.[2]

The strength of these "union-savers" and the advice of Charles Francis Adams caused Andrew to weaken in his opposition to sending commissioners to the Peace Conference.   This yielding on Andrew's part was against the advice of his radical friends, Sumner and the Bird Club,[3] who said to stand firm.   But Adams had written Andrew, January 28, " I am a little afraid that absence would confirm the charge of indifference which is much used against us "; he also expressed the fear that if no authorized rep-

---

[1] *Courier,* Feb. 7, 1861; Schouler, *Massachusetts in the Civil War,* vol. i, p. 43.   The committee named were: Edward Everett, Robert C. Winthrop, Chief Justice Lemuel Shaw, E. S. Toby, Amos A. Lawrence, all of the Constitutional Union party of 1860.

[2] *Cong. Globe,* 36 cong., 2 sess., p. 862.   It was said that many of the signatures were fraudulent.   The *Sumner MSS,* February 13-21, had several letters to this effect.   There was one from John A. Andrew passing on J. M. Forbes' report of a rascal who boasted of signing the petition fourteen times.   Also, M. P. Kennard, an excellent citizen and business man, wrote from Boston: " The petition was placed in the lobby of our post office, under the charge of a crier, who saluted everyone who passed with, ' Sign this petition?'—and it was thoughtlessly signed by men and boys, native and foreign."   Sumner, *Works,* vol. v, p. 477.   The *Advertiser,* February 23, 1861, also said the signers were uninformed as to the nature of the scheme; similarly, Springfield *Republican,* Jan. 28, 1861.   It will be noted that this is all partisan testimony, yet it is so universal as to merit notice.   On the other hand, it must be said that hope of solution through compromise undoubtedly appealed to the people.   This Rhodes has conclusively shown, *History of the United States,* vol. iii, p. 261, note 2.

[3] The Bird Club was a group of men who dined together Saturdays at two; they were not an organized body, but a group of congenial men, anti-slavery in sympathy, who talked things over.   *Cf. infra,* appendix ii, p. 207, note 5.

resentative should come, there would be " a volunteer representation." [1]   Therefore, when resolutions approving the
Crittenden plan were about to be introduced into the state
senate, Andrew asked Dr. Robert T. Davis to rush through
the legislature a resolution which should authorize the governor to appoint commissioners to the proposed Peace Conference.[2]   In defense of this action Andrew wrote F. W.
Bird: " It is of much less importance what is done, than
it is that the thing done should be rightly directed in its
manner, and should be under the right auspices." [3]   The
commissioners were authorized and appointed February 5.
On February 8 the house resolved " that Massachusetts is
unalterably opposed to incorporating into the constitution
of the United States the proposition known as the Crittenden Compromise," and " that our commissioners at Washington are hereby instructed to use every effort to prevent
the adoption of the Crittenden Compromise, or any similar
proposition by the Convention now in session in Washington." [4]

Naturally any concession was loudly attacked by the
radical anti-slavery men and Abolitionists. Garrison voiced
their sentiments when he said:

Personal integrity and straightforward regard for the right
can allow no temptation to make them swerve a hair's breadth

[1] William Claflin wrote Sumner, Feb. 7, 1861: " When it was certain
that our northern border states were going in, I could not see how we
were to stay out. The middle states would be strengthened by sending
a firm delegation from Massachusetts."

[2] *Acts and Resolves*, 1861, chap. vii, p. 537. The commissioners were:
Hon. John Z. Goodrich, Hon. Charles Allen, Hon. George S. Boutwell,
Hon. Francis B. Crowninshield, Theophilus P. Chandler, John M.
Forbes, Richard P. Waters.

[3] Pearson, *Life of Andrew*, vol. i, pp. 155-156.

[4] *Mass. House Leg. Doc.*, 1861, no. 63.

from the line of duty; for they are of more consequence than all the compacts and constitutions ever made. Disregardful of this, the doctrine that " the end justifies the means," or that " we cannot always do what seems absolutely best," becomes the doctrine of devils.[1]

Nevertheless even Sumner made a concession. He wrote to Dr. Howe, January 17, 1861:

I do not speak, for such a speech as I should make would be seized by the conservative press, and be made the apology for the conduct of the slave states. To a member of the house who inquired what " concession " I was willing to make, I said, " There is one: I will consent to be silent yet a little longer." [2]

In general, however, there was a willingness to confer. It was even hoped that the process of electing and holding a convention and discussing the matters at issue might help to inform the people, to remove misunderstandings, and to smooth the way to lasting peace between the sections.[3] At any rate a " freer interchange of ideas from different parts of the union would exercise a beneficial influence."[4] But the amendment before Congress was quite different; for if the constitutional amendment could empower Congress to consider slaves property south of Missouri, it might consider them such north of $36° 30'$,[5] which would be

[1] *Liberator*, March 8, 1861. Also Worcester *Spy*, Jan. 30, 1861: " Nothing can secure peace that does not put an end to slavery propagandism."

[2] Pierce, *Life of Sumner*, vol. iv, p. 9.

[3] This particular sentiment is from the Springfield *Republican*, Feb. 16, 1861.

[4] *Courier*, Feb. 21, 1861. Also view expressed in Forbes' report to Andrew, Forbes, *Reminiscences*, vol. ii, p. 95.

[5] Springfield *Republican*, Jan. 28, 1861; Worcester *Spy*, Jan. 30, 1861; *Advertiser*, Jan. 18, 1861.

the very thing that Massachusetts had just voted should not be done, namely, that slavery should not be extended to the territories. A conference, however, would serve a purpose: through it time could be gained until Lincoln could put forth his policy.[1]

The third disputed point, namely, the repeal of the Personal Liberty Law,[2] concerned Massachusetts more directly. This law had been a source of contention from the time it was passed in 1855.[3] Its purpose was to protect free negroes from being put into bondage under cover of the Fugitive Slave Law; its effect, its opponents said, was to nullify that law.[4] Moreover, since the Personal Liberty Law was a particular grievance to the South,[5] the non-Republican elements of Massachusetts were active for its repeal. Already Governor Banks had expressed a conservative position; in his valedictory he said:

It is not my purpose to defend the constitutionality of the

[1] Forbes, *Letters and Recollections*, vol. i, p. 198, *Reminiscences*, vol. ii, pp. 101, 102, " We killed three weeks"; also Worcester *Spy*, Feb. 28, and *Courier*, Feb. 21, 1861.

[2] Called by opponents " An act to prevent the authorities of the United States from executing the Fugitive Slave Law within the territory of Massachusetts." *Courier*, Jan. 14, 1860.

[3] *General Statutes of Massachusetts, 1860*, ch. cxliv, esp. § 19. Pearson, *op. cit.*, vol. i, pp. 79-90, gives a full and interesting account of how John A. Andrew came into prominence in the legislature through his able defence of this law.

[4] *Courier*, January 14 and February 2, 1860; *Post*, January 17, 1860.

[5] *Life and Letters of George Ticknor*, vol. ii, p. 430: " This is the main, substantial ground of this complaint. But not the only or chief ground." And the Worcester *Spy*, October 1, 1860:

    " *Reporter*—What do you intend doing in the case of Lincoln's election?

    Mr. Toombs of Georgia—Resist him.

    Reporter—Without waiting for an overt act?

    Mr. Toombs—We have overt act enough already; the personal-liberty bills are sufficient."

Fugitive-slave Act. The omission of a provision for jury trial, however harsh and cruel, cannot in any event be supplied by state legislation. While I am constrained to doubt the right of this state to enact such laws, I do not admit that, in any just sense, it is a violation of the national compact. It is only when unconstitutional legislation is enforced by executive authority, that it assumes that character, and no such result has occurred in this State . . . I cannot but regard the maintenance of a statute [such as the Personal Liberty Law], although it may be within the extreme limits of constitutional power, which is so unnecessary to the public service and so detrimental to the public peace, as an inexcusable public wrong. I hope, by common consent, it may be removed from the statute-book, and such guaranties as individual freedom demands be sought in new legislation.[1]

Such was, also, the desire of the Constitutional Union group: Edward Everett, Benjamin R. Curtis, George Ticknor, Amos A. Lawrence, and several others, met at the house of William Appleton and appointed a committee, who presented to the people of Massachusetts an address which demanded conciliation.[2]

---

[1] *Senate Documents*, 1861, no. i, pp. 29, 31.

[2] *Winthrop MSS*, to Judge Clifford, December 3, 1860. The signers of this address were: Lemuel Shaw (recent chief justice of Massachusetts Supreme Court), H. J. Gardner (governor of Massachusetts under the American party), B. R. Curtis, George Ticknor and Levi Lincoln (Constitutional Union group of 1860), Jared Sparks, Theophilus Parsons (Professor of Law at Harvard), George Peabody (merchant), J. G. Abbott (Democrat), also George Ashmun (Whig 1850, Republican 1860). They were characterized by a Sumner correspondent as "either old Whigs or Democrats or those who have joined the Republican ranks at the eleventh hour, out of love, it may be, for the loaves and fishes. . . . I believe these men, if they can succeed in revolutionizing the states with regard to the Fugitive Slave Act, will be equally as ready to dissipate you on the first opportunity as they are now to repeal the Personal Liberty Law." From O. W. Allen, December 19, 1860. Similarly from William Claflin, president of the Massa-

But such was not the position of Governor Andrew; in his inaugural he had taken another stand. He argued:

There can be no doubt that the first and most sacred duty of government is to protect the lives and liberties of subjects.   I believe that every person who is *prima facie* free, being in possession of his liberty and claiming title thereto; that every parent being in possession of his child; or guardian having custody of his minor ward, has a right to a judicial vindication of his rights in that regard, whenever and wherever they are practically drawn in question.   And I do not think that a certificate issued to authorize a person from California to seize and carry away, as and for his fugitive apprentice, the child of a white inhabitant of Massachusetts, . . . can bar the right of such a child or parent to a determination by a competent tribunal, of the right of the child to be retained in this community. . . . So, too, I deny that a certificate so issued to a person from Massachusetts, authorizing him to *seize* and carry away, as and for his fugitive apprentice, the slave of an inhabitant of Georgia, . . . can bar the right of such master to determine by a competent tribunal, of his right to retain his slave under the local law of Georgia. . . . And the right of a person to reclaim an alleged fugitive from his service must always be subordinate to the original, prior, indefeasible right of every freeman to his liberty,—to its preservation, to its instant and constant assertion, and to all the defences of it which pertain to the institutions of Common Law. . . . It is a naked question of right between the Commonwealth and its subjects. . . . Supposing, however, that our legislation in this behalf is founded in mistake, the Legislature will only have endeavored to perform this duty toward the citizen, whom they are bound to shield from unlawful harm.   The

chusetts senate, February 7, 1861. John Murray Forbes also commented: "The good old gentlemen who represent as they think the utter respectability of Massachusetts have made this manifesto on the personal liberty bills on which this whole argument evidently turns on expediency." December 22, 1860.

power to obtain the judgment of the Court affords ample redress to all claimants.[1]

It was against this position of Andrew that remonstrance was made. Supporters of Andrew, on the other hand, maintained that the views of the law held by the Southerners were incorrect; and that therefore to repeal the law in compliance with their demands would be improper concession.[2] The Republican press divided. Many argued that it would be better that the law in question should be removed from the statute book by a simple repeal, and that the state should not seek to qualify and explain that which was subject to such misconstruction.[3] The Abolitionists, of course, declared that this was saying peace where there was no peace, putting new wine into old bottles, and serving two masters.[4] But very many Republicans believed that if the laws were made the occasion or the pretense for disturbing friendly relations between the sections, and if they were incapable of substantial good, they ought to be repealed;[5] and finally Andrew gave up his firm stand. He saw, also, that the Hunkers were trying to use the laws to split the Republican

[1] *Senate Documents*, 1861, no. ii, pp. 32-35.

[2] Worcester *Spy*, January 8, 1861; and the *Advertiser*, November 19, 1860, said the governor of Georgia quoted as grievances sections of our law which had been repealed, and quoted as a New York law a bill which had never been passed.

[3] *Advertiser*, Feb. 22 and Mar. 28, 1861; Springfield *Republican*, Nov. 24, 1860; E. Littell in the *Advertiser* suggested the necessity of repeal as a simple tribute to the Union men in Virginia, Maryland, Kentucky, and Tennessee. *Sumner MSS*, from E. Littell, Feb. 25, 1861.

[4] Clark, *Secession, Concession, or Self-Possession* (pam.), p. 27.

[5] Thomas, *Suggestions upon the Personal Liberty Law* (pam.), pp. 13, 14; also *Advertiser*, Feb. 22, 1861. Forbes, *Letters* (*Supplementary*), vol. i, p. 235, to Charles F. Adams, Jan. 20, 1861: "If repeal of Personal Liberty Laws will conciliate Maryland so that she will stay with the North and defend the capital, it may be well to attempt it."

party;[1] therefore he aided the committee on federal relations to discover a course upon which both elements could unite.[2] In the end the following enactment was made which practically annulled the laws:

Nothing contained in the statutes of the Commonwealth shall be construed to authorize the taking of any person out of the custody of the United States marshal, or his deputy, holding him by legal and sufficient process, issued by any court or magistrate of competent jurisdiction, *provided, however,* that this shall not affect the authority of the supreme judicial court, or the justices, in accordance with the provisions of the constitution of the United States, and of this Commonwealth, to investigate and determine upon the validity and legal effect of any process which may be relied on to defeat the writ, or any other matters properly arising.[3]

Thus although there was some opposition to compromise measures, there was generally a " magnanimous " sentiment which was willing to listen to plans of conciliation.[4] The

[1] *Cf. supra*, p. 50.

[2] The remonstrance sent by the meeting at the Appleton house was referred to this committee on federal relations about fugitive slaves, *etc.* Pearson, *Life of Andrew*, vol. i, pp. 165-166 and note.

[3] *Laws and Resolves*, 1861, ch. xci, § 3, pp. 398-399 (March 25, 1861). Criticism still continued thus: " The Personal Liberty Laws have been modified to be of no effect. It would have been better to have repealed them to prevent misapprehension."—*Advertiser*, Mar. 28, 1861.

[4] The *Advertiser* quoted the following defense: " If we have to go to battle, will it not have been well for us to be able to say that we acted magnanimously, and did all that was possible for conciliation?" Jan. 30, 1861.

Holmes' lines, from " Brother Jonathan's Lament for Sister Carolina," published in the *Atlantic* (May, 1861), vol. vii, p. 613, were evidently prompted by the same spirit:

" You were always too ready to fire at a touch;
But we said, ' She is hasty,—she does not mean much.'
We have scowled, when you uttered some turbulent threat;
But Friendship still whispered, ' Forgive and forget!'"

conciliatory spirit, however, was supplemented by financial interests: a quarrel with the South was disturbing to business, therefore compromise![1]   Some, on the other hand, thought the financial situation would show the Southerners their folly: the *Advertiser*, with its finger on the financial pulse, said, " There is . . . a strong impression in stock circles in Wall Street that the political crisis is to end within a short time ";[2] and even so late as March 20 opinion appeared to be hopeful of continued peace.   Moreover the same optimism which in November had asserted that secession was merely a threat now held the present state of affairs to be but temporary.   The antislavery *Spy,* for example, prophesied that the tempest of unreasonable passion would spend its force and subside, for it held that Jefferson Davis and others had " intended only a political game, which was to result in destroying the Republican party, and establishing themselves at the head of a party which would control the government ".[3]   Consequently when Maryland and Delaware were saved to the Union, the progress in secession was considered to have reached its high water mark, from which it must recede from then on.[4]   On the other hand the pro-slavery *Courier* said that the states would resume their places in the Union if encouraged to do so by the action of

[1] *Cf. supra,* pp. 47-49.

[2] *Advertiser,* Jan. 19, 1861.

[3] January 12, 1861. It was, however, acknowledged by some to be a scheme of long standing brought forward at the opportune time—the change of administration. And the Springfield *Republican,* January 8, 1861, said: " The movements for the extension of slavery have come from politicians, being designed to retain the control of the general government." Similarly the *Advertiser,* Dec. 18, the *Courier,* Dec. 3, the Springfield *Republican,* Dec. 15, 1860, and *Spy,* Jan. 16, 1861.

[4] Springfield *Republican,* June 19, 1861 : " Breezes may blow and there may be a great tumult in the waters, but the tide will be running out all the time."

the North.[1]   Such confidence from opposing parties would naturally encourage compromise.

Political leaders, however, were not deceived.   Andrew's visit to Washington in December had convinced him of the seriousness of the situation; his inaugural showed a consciousness of possible imminent war.   At the end he said: " The people of Massachusetts, confiding in the patriotism of their brethren in other States, accept this issue, and respond, in the words of Jackson, *The Federal Union, it must be preserved!* " [2]   In this address, he also made a point of military preparation: he maintained the advisability of placing the militia on a footing of activity, that the state might be ready without delay to contribute her share of force at any exigency of public danger, for such preparedness alone could in the long run avert the creation of standing armies.[3]   This statement, however, caused no particular comment, because the need of military preparation was not recognized by the people, and because the statement was sufficiently judicious in phrasing to avoid attracting attention.   Yet Andrew was awake to the ultimate possibilities and exigencies: in fact, on his inauguration day, he had received a letter from Adams warning him of danger to the Federal Capital, and advising that state legislatures should make military preparations at once and quietly.

These instructions were carried out immediately.   Messengers were sent to the governors of the New England states urging them to prepare for a coming crisis; and on January 16 William Schouler, adjutant-general, was directed (by Andrew) to issue General Order No. 4, which opened as follows: " Events which have recently occurred,

---

[1] March 28, 1861.

[2] *Senate Documents*, 1861, no. 2, p. 46.

[3] *Ibid.*, p. 9.

and are now in progress, require that Massachusetts should be at all times ready to furnish her quota upon any requisition of the President of the United States, to aid in the maintenance of the laws and the peace of the Union." The order provided for correcting the rolls of the militia companies and filling the vacancies " by men ready for any public exigency which may arise." [1]

Although the order was a part of the governor's policy of preparation for a coming emergency, it was in answer to the report which the adjutant-general had made to Governor Banks on December 31, which asked for such authority.[2] Banks had retired from office four days after the report was printed. This order, therefore, appeared in the light of unfinished business, and, as such, attracted less attention than it otherwise might have done.

Nevertheless the partisan press commended and condemned. The *Advertiser* was satisfied that the necessities of the case could be met without bringing Massachusetts forward obtrusively or offensively; the *Courier,* on the other hand, claimed that citizen soldiery were entitled to know what were the exigencies and objects of such extraordinary proceedings.[3] In the meantime the new legislature, on January 11, referred to its committee on federal relations a resolution to the effect that the universal sentiment of the people of Massachusetts was " that the President should enforce the execution of the laws of the United States, defend the Union, protect national property "; and thereafter followed a series of military resolutions and acts which were part of the daily business until the close of the session, April 11.

[1] The order is printed in full in Schouler, *History of Massachusetts in the Civil War*, vol. i, p. 21.

[2] *Ibid.*, pp. 18, 19.

[3] January 18, 1861. The *Post* was silent on this subject until after the presidential inauguration.

Indeed, so swift were the preparations that by January 23 the governor informed the house that Colonel Jones tendered the Sixth regiment for immediate service, if required.

Upon this there appeared numerous protests from all parties, from administration as well as from anti-administration papers. The Springfield *Republican* published a long article entitled, "Arming the North against the South," which protested against inflaming the popular mind and distracting the popular attention from the ordinary pursuits of private life; it did not believe there was anything in present circumstances, or future probabilities, to justify exasperating the South needlessly by putting the New England states on a war footing.[1] The *Courier* declared: "All this is anti-republican, anti-democratic,—in fact, mere despotism, and an entire departure from the principles, spirit and usage of our free institutions."[2]

The special point of attack was a bill rescinding the act of 1858 which had reduced both the number of companies in the militia and the number of men in each company. In other words there was protest because of the traditional abhorrence for a large and powerful militia, or anything suggestive of a standing army. The criticism of the *Advertiser*, for example, was not directed against the improvement of the militia, but against the adoption of a measure which provided for a permanent increase in. it. Yet whatever criticisms the *Advertiser* made on the method adopted, all its discussions of the militia were distinct from its discussions of coercion of the South; for instance, it answered Captain Manning of Salem, as follows:

The truth is, Captain Manning makes the mistake . . . in supposing that it is proposed to march an army to the con-

[1] January 24, 1861.
[2] January 21, 1861.

quest of the South. . . . No one has the slightest reason to suppose that Mr. Lincoln will pursue any except a strictly defensive policy—holding the property of the government, defending it from attack, and collecting the revenue as is his duty to do.[1]

After January, however, the *Advertiser* was silent on the militia question. The *Courier* and *Post* said but little: the former criticized Order No. 7, which summoned the militia to hold itself in readiness for defense of the Federal Capital when the Peace Conference was in session in Washington; [2] and the *Post*, in March, said that by war and war alone could the Massachusetts politicians hope to maintain their party in power upon the basis of the Chicago platform.[3] A letter published in the *Post* some two weeks later said that the Southern brethren had become alarmed after the John Brown episode and recent military preparations, and that they had withdrawn and desired to be let alone.[4] This and the comment of the Springfield *Republican* that the " Montgomery cabinet is reported to be laughing over what it considers the weak preparations for war at the North ",[5] are the only newspaper evidence of any belief that military preparations in Massachusetts had anything to do with the crisis.

Thus on the whole it would appear that the opposition to military measures was due to a general failure to comprehend the possible imminence of war. Even though

---

[1] Jan. 29, 1861, in answer to the protests of Captain Manning of the Salem Light Artillery. This was the only militia company of the state that protested against the new measures. Pearson, *Life of Andrew*, vol. i, p. 147 and note 2.

[2] Feb. 8, 1861.

[3] *Post*, March 14, 1861.

[4] *Post*, March 27, 1861.

[5] April 17, 1861.

threats against Washington were noted in the press,[1] and even though the Peace Conference failed, nevertheless the Springfield *Republican*, as late as April 6, claimed to believe that although there might be " a new disunion flurry " yet there was possibility of peace.[2] Reports of plans for the taking of Fort Pickens and Fort Sumter did not receive serious attention, for, it was argued, any rash step on the part of South Carolina would put her in the wrong. Indeed, from the very beginning, it was held to be incredible that the Southern states could long persevere in a policy which would inflict untold commercial distress on their own community. And, after the inauguration of Lincoln, there was a sense of security, because of the belief in the firm yet peaceable policy of the new administration.[3] It was indeed hard for a people to conceive of something of which they had no experience: civil war was new.[4]

When the presidential election was over, then the majority believed disunion improbable; when disunion became

---

[1] Worcester *Spy*, Jan. 15 and Feb. 2, 1861; *Advertiser*, Feb. 4, 1861.

[2] Amos A. Lawrence wrote J. J. Crittenden, Dec. 29, 1860: " Nine out of ten of our people would laugh if told that blood must be shed." Yet to the contrary on Dec. 29, 1860, the *Pilot* had said: " It is impossible not to see Civil War in the distance," and similarly *Winthrop MSS*, to J. P. Kennedy, Dec. 27, 1860; and Francis J. Parker in the Boston *Mercury* quoted in the Worcester *Spy*, Dec. 11, 1860. But these last were the minority, the one out of ten.

[3] Springfield *Republican*, March 6, 1861; *Courier*, March 5, 1861; *Post*, March 5 and 16, 1861. Yet Warrington now (as the *Pilot* and Winthrop in December, 1860) wrote: " It is more evident every day that there is an irrepressible conflict which will compel a separation eventually."—Springfield *Republican*, April 6, 1861.

[4] Edward L. Pierce remarks that the correspondents of Sumner, whether for or against concession, were groping in darkness and uncertainty, " but none foresaw great armies facing each other."—*Life of Sumner*, vol. iv, p. 22. And C. F. Adams, *Autobiography* (pp. 69-70): " But of the tremendous nature of that future, we then had no conception."

a fact, they believed it temporary. Naturally they were
more or less willing to conciliate; conciliation was an American political habit, and moreover, it was a generous policy.
Yet above all else Union and the authority of the government must stand. They hoped that time would bring about
a peaceable and satisfactory solution.

CHAPTER III

THE DEFENSE OF THE UNION

WITH the fall of Sumter on April 12 the whole country was awakened. Massachusetts, in particular, no longer left adjustment to time; within a week five Massachusetts regiments started South.[1] Boston banks desired to increase the resources of the state and aid the preparations of the North; they, therefore, offered to loan money to the governor without security.[2] In truth

the guns of South Carolina battered down a great deal more than the walls of the forts,—party divisions and prejudices, personal interests, private or social differences all fell before them. The whole North was heartily united, and there was but one feeling and one will among them all. It was not that their passions were aroused . . . but their self-respect, their intelligent and conservative love of order, government, and law, all their instinctive love of liberty, and their sense of

[1] The regiments were (in the order of their going), the 3d, 4th, 6th, 8th, 5th. Major Cook's Light Artillery and the Third Battalion of Rifles went also. For the description of the departure of these regiments, see the adjutant-general's account: Schouler, *History of Massachusetts*, vol. i, ch. ii; also Pearson, *Life of Andrew*, vol. i, ch. v, vi and viii; *Journal and Letters* of Samuel G. Howe, vol. ii, p. 481; and the Boston *Journal*, April 18-22, 1861.

[2] Worcester *Spy*, April 18, 1861.—The Suffolk Bank offered Gov. Andrew $100,000 and the Secretary of the U. S. Treasury $100,000. The Webster Bank voted a loan of $50,000 to the state. Schouler, *History of Massachusetts*, vol. i, p. 53.—Boston banks offered $3,600,000 to the state.

responsibility for the safety of the blessings of freedom and popular government, were stirred to their very depth.[1]

In the words of the press, " The traitorous blow struck at the flag roused the mercantile community as well as the rest ";[2] and Amos A. Lawrence could write J. J. Crittenden on April 16:

You have but a faint idea of the indignation which has seized the people since the defeat of Anderson. Every man wishes to be a volunteer. Business is suspended, political asperities have ceased and we all stand as one man for the government. . . . Our friends in Kentucky may rely on it the Government will be sustained.[3]

The next event, the firing on the Sixth regiment in Baltimore, blew the flame of indignation to white heat. This was a direct attack on fellow-citizens of Massachusetts. The mass of the people were thoroughly convinced that if things had come to this pass no quarter should be given.[4]

---

[1] Norton, *Letters*, vol. i, p. 234, to A. H. Clough, May 27, 1861. Also the Worcester *Spy*, April 27, 1861: "At once partisan differences were forgotten, partisan antagonism melted away, the hearts of the people united in a mighty cheer for the old star spangled banner and in a mighty purpose to maintain our republican institutions against the conspirator that would destroy them."

[2] *Advertiser*, April 17, 1861. Similarly the *Post*, June 18, said: " We may not make money for a season—perhaps we have thought too much of money in times past—but we are united . . . it [war] is to be pursued until treason is rooted out and crushed."

[3] *Lawrence MSS*, April 16, 1861.

[4] A broadside of the time by Charles S. Smith expressed the popular sentiment while stirring it:

" They have felt the Southerner's insults, they have borne his bitter taunts,
They have listened without answer to his weak and childish vaunts;
Till the Nation's flag was trampled on, they patiently forebore;
But now they strike for Freedom—*and the slain at Baltimore!*"

And finally the last of the critics who blamed the administration for the disaster, who said that sending reinforce-
ments to Sumter threatened coercion, and who saw no sufficient cause for war, feeling that it would sacrifice lives
and property and settle nothing,[1] — those critics were
silenced by the issuing of letters of marque and reprisal
from Montgomery. The *Courier* then declared, " There
will be no more talk about rights or wrongs; that day is
happily past, for rights and wrongs have been swallowed
up in the enormous wrong committed by the blood-stained
traitors of Montgomery. Hereafter *we act*." [2]

Of this united sentiment Sumner wrote: " I never believed that the North would be practically divided when
the conflict came; but I did not expect the ferocious unity
and high-strung determination which are now witnessed." [3]
And even the Abolitionists were quiet for a time. Garrison wrote on April 23, " Let us all stand aside when the
North is rushing like a tornado in the right direction " [4]
and Wendell Phillips, who on April 9 had spoken for disunion, on the 21st said:

[1] *Courier*, April 13 and 16, 1861; also Lunt, *The Origin of the Late
War*, p. 451.

[2] *Courier*, April 20, 1861. Also Edward Everett, at the Academy of
Music in New York, July 4, 1861, took the same stand: "They have
broken the constitution by raising armies and issuing letters of marque."
Works, vol. iv, p. 353.

[3] Pierce, *Life of Sumner*, vol. iv, p. 37.

[4] Garrison papers, April 23, 1861, to Oliver Johnson. On the 19th he
had written Johnson: "Now that civil war has begun, and a whirl-
wind of violence and excitement is to sweep through the country,
every day increasing in intensity until its bloodiest culmination, it is
for the abolitionists to 'stand still, and see the salvation of God,'
rather than attempt to add anything to the general commotion. It is
no time for minute criticism of Lincoln, Republicanism, or even the
other parties, now that they are fusing for a death grapple with the
Southern slave oligarchy; for they are instruments in the hands of
God to carry forward and help achieve the great object of emancipation, for which we have so long been striving."

The only mistake I have made was in supposing Massachusetts wholly choked with cotton dust and cankered with gold. . . . The struggle now is, not of opinion, but of civilization. . . . The South opened with a cannon-shot, and Lincoln showed himself at the door. The war is not of aggression, but of self-defence; and Washington becomes the Thermopylae of liberty and justice. Rather than surrender it, cover every foot of ground with a living man. Guard it with a million men, and empty our bank-vaults to pay them. Proclaim that the North is under the stars and stripes, and no man is in chains.[1]

Thus, although he did not forget his cherished cause, he was now for the Union.

The unanimity of sentiment in which all partisan differences were forgotten was shown in Union meetings held in Boston and Cambridge. Conservatives and Breckinridge Democrats, all stood for the cause of Union; George S. Hillard of the *Courier* was one of the speakers at the Washington Elm meeting; and Benjamin F. Hallett, who had been a seceder at the Baltimore convention, followed Edward Everett at the Chester Square flag-raising. To this meeting Everett said:

Fidelity to the Union blazes from its stars: allegiance to the Government under which we live is wrapped within its folds. We set up this standard, my friends, not as a matter of idle display, but as an expressive indication, that, in the migthy struggle which has been forced upon us, we are of one heart and of one mind—that the Government of the Country must be sustained. . . . We forget that we ever had been partisans;

[1] In Theodore Parker's Church, Boston, quoted in the *Liberator*, Apr. 26, 1861. The New York *Tribune*, Aug. 20, 1862, quoted Phillips as saying: "Sumter changed the whole question." Elsewhere Abolitionists explained that the earlier disunion agitation of the Abolitionists was justified by their cause, while the move on the part of the South was condemned by its cause.

we remember only that we are American and that our country is in peril.[1]

Nowhere was there any mention of slavery, except among the radical Abolitionists.[2]　Even Andrew, devotedly anti-slavery, submerged his cherished cause.[3]　In his address to the special session of the legislature, May 14, he said:

This is no war of sections,—no war of North or South.　It is waged to avenge no former wrongs, nor to propitiate ancient griefs or memories of conflict.　It is the struggle of the People to vindicate their own rights, to retain and invigorate the institutions of their fathers,—the majestic effort of a National Government to vindicate its power and execute its functions for the welfare and happiness of the whole,—and therefore while I do not forget, I will not name to-day that "*subtle poison*" which has lurked always in our national system.[4]

The people generally, in all probability, as John Murray Forbes declared, "had no clear conception of the evils of slavery, nor were all aware that this inherited curse was at the bottom of the strife";[5] but all did understand the attack on the Union and were stirred by it.　It was undoubtedly with truth, therefore, that the Springfield *Republican* in August asserted that ninety-nine in every one hundred of the people of Massachusetts were in favor of Union and were loyal supporters of the government.[6]

How large a portion were really apart from the popular

---

[1] Everett, *Works*, vol. iv, p. 326; and even the *Post* (Apr. 22, 1861) said: "Let every man's motto be, 'I AM WITH MY COUNTRY AND FOR MY COUNTRY UNDER ALL CIRCUMSTANCES AND IN EVERY CONTINGENCY.'"

[2] *Cf. infra*, ch. iv, p. 90.

[3] Andrew got his cue from Washington.—Pearson, *Life of Andrew*, vol. i, p. 249.

[4] *Senate Documents*, extra sess., 1861, no. 2, pp. 4-5.

[5] Forbes, *Letters and Recollections*, vol. i, p. 202.

[6] Aug. 30, 1861.

enthusiasm is hard to determine, for it was the safer or more comfortable policy for them to conceal their views. And now that the war is over and the judgment of history defends the policy of the administration, the minority generally prefer to forget their mistaken judgment.

A few incidents of violence toward disloyalty are nevertheless recorded. In Haverhill a certain Ambrose L. Kimball, editor and publisher of a journal of limited circulation called the *Essex County Democrat*, offended the loyal citizens by his persistent hostility to the government. He was taken from his house, tarred and feathered, and carried on a rail over into Bradford, where he was made to kneel and promise to print no more treason.[1] Two similar incidents occurred in the little town of Wales: one Farrington was carried on a rail, and a certain Miller was ridden head to tail on a blind horse.[2] Near Worcester, Mr. Bond of Boylston gathered thirty friends in his defense against a threatened second visit by loyalist neighbors.[3] A Mr. Curtis was compelled to nail a flag to his house.[4] There were also

[1] *Courier* and Worcester *Spy*, Aug. 21, 1861. (Newspaper offices were destroyed in Concord, N. H., and Bangor, Maine. *Advertiser*, Aug. 14, 1861.)

[2] Springfield *Republican*, May 13, 1861.

[3] Worcester *Spy*, Oct. 22, 1861. The Bonds were charged with firing a salute after the defeat at Bull Run.

[4] Testimony of a son of Mr. Curtis, who now (1914) lives on the farm. A humorous story is told in South Hadley. A stranger who moved to the town lived by himself and received many letters. He was suspected of being in league with the rebels. In his absence neighbors found a heavy box in his wood-shed. They were convinced that arms and ammunition were being collected to send South. A day or two later a mob collected at the post-office and went to his house. Accusations and threats were so violent it was some time before he learned what they wanted. Then he opened his house, his letters and the box. Around the sitting-room were several chess-boards; the correspondence concerned these games of chess. The box contained books. The mob dispersed. This incident was told by Miss Sophie Eastman, contemporary.

a few incidents of whole towns that were rebellious; for example, Southwick, a town in Hampden County, refused by vote of 56 to 18 to appropriate $2000 for volunteers,[1] and in Agawam the selectmen refused to call a town meeting. In the latter case a meeting was finally called by a justice of the peace and money was appropriated for volunteers and the support of their families.[2] But when these cases are enumerated we have exhausted the records. It would seem therefore that in the early months of the war outspoken opponents of the administration and open sympathizers with rebellion were few and far between.[3]

But, after four or five months, ardor and enthusiasm cooled and it was possible to mention compromise. For various reasons there were numerous not unqualified supporters of the war.[4] Some, undoubtedly, like the farmers of Maine, felt the whole affair was no concern of theirs; there were besides a number who conscientiously believed in state rights, the most extreme holding that the government had no right to exercise coercion under any circumstances. J. P. Blanchard, pamphleteer for this faction, argued:

Holding slaves as property is a great and oppressive wrong, but, there being no power in the Constitution to remedy that wrong, it is reserved to the States who act in the case for

[1] Springfield *Republican*, May 14, 1861.

[2] *Ibid.*, May 11, 1861.

[3] Hawthorne could be counted among them. He wrote, May 26: "I must say that I rejoice that the old Union is smashed. We never were one people, and never really had a country since the Constitution was formed." Bridge, *Personal Recollections of Hawthorne*, p. 169.

[4] *E. g.*, the *Pilot*, Aug. 16, 1861: "We would bear the sword and the olive branch together. We should keep our armies in the field and our powder dry, but also keep our hearts open to rational terms of compromise."

themselves; and, in like manner, there being no provision in the Constitution either to permit or prohibit secession, it is reserved power to the States, the execution of which, right or wrong, each state must decide for itself. The war, therefore, to prevent or recover this secession by force, is not only ineffectual, and for a wrong purpose, but a gross usurpation of ungranted power.[1]

There were moreover a great many neutrals. They were loyal to the Union because of their reverence for the Constitution, but their hatred for the Abolitionists was so strong that they were loath even to join themselves to the Republicans, for they felt that the war had resulted in a measure from Abolitionist agitation and that the Republicans were aiding these reformers by prosecuting the war. At the same time, there were extreme Abolitionists who were not eager to return to a union with slave holders.[2] And finally there were pro-slavery sympathizers who felt that, though the war was nominally for the Union, slavery was involved, and who would not fight to abolish slavery.

Some of the pro-slavery faction were directly interested financially in the system: the South, in fact, was the great market for various manufactured products of New England;[3] the shoe factories around Danvers, for example, made shoes for the slaves in the South; furthermore merchants or those building railroads, had taken mortgages on

[1] Blanchard, *The War of Secession* (pam.), p. 9.

[2] For example, a strong-minded woman coming out of Music Hall on a day when news of Union triumph had come, is reported to have "groaned out": "If things are going on in this way, we shall have the old government back again and all the Slave States, just as they were before, and what will become of emancipation?" *Courier*, March 3 and May 6, 1862.

[3] *Cf. supra*, ch. ii.

the slaves and sometimes had become slave owners.[1] There were, also, still other pro-slavery sympathizers who did not condemn the institution of slavery itself; for in 1861 the children of those who remembered the emancipated family servants with affection, still cherished the traditions of slavery at its best, and therefore, sympathized with the Southerner's attitude toward it.[2]

In the summer of 1861, however, these lukewarm factions were ineffective, enthusiasm for Union was paramount and any mention of compromise only called forth expressions of Union sentiment and strengthened the support of the war. The most of the public believed, as did Lowell, that conciliation after reverses would " put the party of law and loyalty in the wrong and would mean disunion "; they believed, moreover, that discussion would give the rebels time to consolidate their organization.[3] And there were those who scorned compromise because they were confident of easy victory, realizing neither the determination nor the resources of the South.[4] But in the last analysis the senti-

---

[1] Reminiscence of Frank B. Sanborn. Mr. Sanborn said he knew of merchants who, in payment for goods, had taken mortgages on plantations and slaves, and consequently wanted difficulties patched up. He, however, declined to give the names.

[2] Slaves had been held in Massachusetts until 1783, when the court decided that the phrase of the Constitution declaring " all men are born free and equal" annulled the master's right to the labor of his slave. Jeremiah Page, of Danvers, was the last slave-owner of Massachusetts. The late Miss Ann Page described the attitude of her father and other people of her acquaintance. Her descriptions contributed largely to the above conclusions.

[3] Lowell, " Pickens and Stealin's Rebellion," *Atlantic* (June, 1861), vol. vii, p. 760.

[4] This confidence lasted into 1862. Worcester *Spy*, Feb. 13 and Nov. 12, 1862; the *Post*, May 8, 1862, "The rebellion is crumbling"; the Springfield *Republican*, July 15, 1861, Feb. 2, 8, 27, Aug. 20 and May 12, 1862; with the fall of Norfolk it said: "The backbone of the re-

ment of all parties was the same, "The *Union* must be preserved."

At the same time it was emphatically declared that abolition was not the purpose of the war; that the duty of the government was to suppress rebellion and "let slavery take care of itself";[1] for the great purpose of the war was to rescue the government from destruction and uphold the Constitution and the Union. The preservation of this Union was regarded as a sacred trust inherited from the fathers, and for its preservation the people were responsible "to humanity and to Almighty God";[2] indeed both Democrats and Republicans believed confidently that unless the rebellion were shaken from centre to circumference the great experiment of democratic institutions would prove a failure. The existence of the nation was threatened by conspirators who would seek to destroy it because they could not control it.[3] It was therefore the duty of the men of

bellion is broken, and though there may be some fighting yet, the remaining part of the subjugation of the enemy will be comparatively easy." Also Amos A. Lawrence (*MSS*) assured his sister (Mrs. Arnold), on May 27, 1861: "The Union will be maintained and the 'stars and stripes' will wave over our whole seaboard before New Year's, and over the whole country before another New Year's after that. There is no more doubt about it than that the sun will rise."

[1] Springfield *Republican*, June 8, Nov. 13 and 15, 1861, Jan. 9, 1862; *Courier*, May 2, 1861; also Springfield *Republican*, May 23, 1862: "We yield in our hatred of slavery to no man, but the destruction of slavery is not the object for which our armies were brought into the field."

[2] Benjamin F. Thomas in his Faneuil Hall speech, reported in the Worcester *Spy*, Sept. 10, 1866. Similarly, Edward Everett said in Roxbury, May 8, 1861, the war "is for the very existence of the Government; it is a contest in which no good citizen can remain neutral." *Works*, vol. iv, p. 336. And in his Fourth-of-July oration he said the great issues before the country were nothing less than "whether the work of our noble Fathers of the Revolution and Constitutional age shall perish or endure."—*Post*, July 4, 1861; *Works*, vol. iv, p. 405.

[3] C. Hodge, *England and America* (pam.), p. 4; also Forbes, *Letters*

the North to preserve it as an inspiration to all lovers of freedom, and a blessing to mankind.[1]

To champion this cause of Union a big meeting was held in Faneuil Hall on September 9, 1861. Among the vice-presidents were George S. Boutwell, Robert C. Winthrop, Josiah G. Abbott; Republican, Constitutional Unionist and Democrat. Here it was asserted " no matter who carries the flag we follow the stars and stripes ", and it was declared that " no compromise shall lull us to repose." Robert C. Winthrop said: " We must act for the present. . . . Our misguided brethren of the South have left us no other alternative but to fight. Our capital must be defended. Our flag must be sustained, the authority of the government must be vindicated." [2]

It was in this spirit that Benjamin F. Hallett (who had been of the seceders' convention in Baltimore) suggested that party action should be suspended until war was at an end. The simple issue, he said,

is the overthrow or the support of the Government in this whole Union; and while that is the issue, I am not for opposing or obstructing any measure or policy of the administration honestly designed to carry on this war for its great end, viz.: *the re-establishment of the supreme Government of the Union*

and Recollections, vol. ii, p. 74: " The war is not the North against the South, but the people against the aristocracy"; and later Henry Wilson said, *"American slavery must die that the nation may live."*—"The Duty of the Hour," given before the Fraternity of Boston, Oct. 7, 1862.

[1] C. F. Adams in his farewell address said: " We are now the champions of law and republican liberty" (pam., p. 8). The Springfield *Republican*, Nov. 30, 1861, claimed: " The putting down of this gigantic rebellion . . . settles the question touching the strength and weakness of a democratic government for all the nations of the Earth." Similarly, Guild in a pamphlet, *War and Why it Is*, p. 8, held that " the power of self-government is on trial, in our case, before the tribunal of the world."

[2] *Courier*, Sept. 10, 1861; Worcester *Spy*, Sept. 10, 1861.

in all the States and Territories. Until that is done, or it is demonstrated that it cannot be done by force of arms, I belong to no party but the country. . . . *A party nomination can do no good to the country and may do harm. . . . Let Massachusetts be a unit, in support of the Union, and let there be no division as to men in this election.*[1]

Caleb Cushing also added his influence; at Salisbury Beach, on September 17, he said:

Whatever may have been our antecedents, there is no uncertainty as to the duty of every citizen of the United States. . . . In such a time as this to talk of political parties is not the thing. Party now is but the dust in the balance, the foam on the wave in comparison with Union and Liberty.[2]

To this same end the chairman of the state central committee, Democratic, received the following communication:

At a meeting of the state central committee and others, of the Constitutional Union party, held in Boston this day, the undersigned were appointed a committee to confer with the Democratic and Republican parties, in reference to an abandonment of existing party organizations, and the calling of a People's Convention to nominate State officers.[3]

The Democratic convention, however, did not follow this advice. Hallett and Cushing were absent. Though Oliver Stevens moved that they should adjourn without making any nominations, the other faction, led by E. A. Alger, of Lowell, was stronger; a full ticket was nominated, and Isaac Davis was named for governor. The convention had come together in response to the call to those " who

---

[1] *Post*, Sept. 14, 1861.

[2] *Advertiser*, Sept. 19, 1861.

[3] *Post*, Sept. 19, 1861. Report of the Constitutional Union meeting at the Parker House appeared in the *Courier*, Sept. 13, 1861.

believe that the vigorous prosecution of the war should be accompanied by the most liberal proffers of peace," [1] and Judge Wells offered a resolution for calling a convention of one delegate from each congressional district in New England to suggest an amendment to the Federal Constitution acceptable to the North and South, and which would furnish ample guarantee of protection to the rights of the South. The motion was laid on the table; instead the convention resolved that " the Federal Government must and shall be maintained," that " it becomes the imperative duty of every citizen to sustain the administration in a vigorous prosecution of the war as the only means of securing lasting peace." It nevertheless challenged the national administration " to guarantee the right of every state to regulate its domestic affairs in its own way, especially the freedom of the press, the right of personal liberty, the privilege of the writ of habeas corpus and trial by jury." It condemned, furthermore, the Republican party for keeping its party organization. [2]

The call of the Republican convention sounded a very different note; it was to those

who are in favor of union for the support of the Government and for a vigorous prosecution of the war . . . who are determined without reservation to support the constituted authorities in all attempts to restore the sway of the Constitution and the Laws over every portion of the country, . . . for the purpose of testifying to all loyal men throughout the country their unfaltering and persistent purpose to maintain free principles and democratic institutions inherited from our fathers, and thus secure a peace—the only one substantial and permanent, based upon a successful vindication of the supremacy of constitutional law. [3]

[1] *Post*, Aug. 17, 1861.   [2] *Post*, Sept. 19, 1861.
[3] *Advertiser*, Sept. 28, 1861.

The same determination for " permanent, safe and honorable peace " through " the extinction of armed rebellion " was embodied in the resolutions.[1]

Yet another note was struck in the convention by Charles Sumner, who said :

Rebel conspirators have set upon us, and now besiege the National Government. . . .   Bridges are burned.   Railways are disabled.   Steamers and ships seized. . . .   Commerce is hunted on the sea, and property, wherever it can be reached, ruthlessly robbed or destroyed. . . .   In the name of slavery, and nothing else, is all the crime, destruction and ravage perpetrated; and the work still proceeds. . . .   It is often said that the war will make an end of slavery.   This is probable.   But it is surer still that the overthrow of Slavery will mean an end of the war. . . .   Two objects are before us, Union and Peace, each for the sake of the other, and both for the sake of the country; but without Emancipation how can we expect either ?[2]

But the convention was not ready to follow any such doctrines; instead it voted down the resolution of James Freeman Clarke to " welcome any act under the war power which should declare all slaves within the lines of our armies free . . . compensating all loyal owners."[3]   Obviously the Republican party in Massachusetts was not yet ready to stand for emancipation even as a military measure; in fact, the proposition was considered to be ill-timed and out of place.[4]   Instead of supporting a " crusade ", the

[1] *Advertiser*, Oct. 2, 1861.

[2] *Advertiser*, Oct. 2, 1861; Sumner, *Works*, vol. vi, pp. 1-29.

[3] *Advertiser*, Oct. 2, 1861; *Am. Annual Cyclop.*, 1861, p. 453.

[4] Springfield *Republican*, Oct. 2, 1861: " We could not but feel that Mr. Sumner's speech was ill-timed and out of place." *Advertiser*, Oct. 4, 1861: " Neither men nor money will be forthcoming for this war, if once the people are impressed with the belief that the abolition of

convention professed to recognize the demand that was being made for union of all votes in favor of sustaining the national administration.

To that end the convention nominated Edward Dickinson, a Bell-Everett man, for lieutenant-governor, and J. G. Abbott, a Democrat, for attorney-general. The secretary, when informing Dickinson of his nomination, characterized the convention as

all the citizens of the commonwealth who are in favor of union for the support of the government, and for a vigorous prosecution of the war against wicked and unprovoked rebellion, and who are determined in good faith . . . to restore the sway of the Constitution and Laws in all portions of the country.[1]

But the plan failed. Dickinson and Abbott both declined, for they felt that they were being nominated by the Republican convention; in fact, Dickinson described the honor as " gracefully and unexpectedly tendered by a numerous convention composed of men of a political organization of which I am not a member." Later in his letter he said that the great mass of the people were ready to sustain the state administration and its policy if the committees of the political organizations had united in calling a People's convention without distinction of party. He claimed that it was a time when all party organizations and platforms should sink into utter insignificance, and demanded that the national administration and its policy be maintained until "the

slavery and not the defence of the union is the object." Also Adams' *Dana*, vol. ii, p. 260: "He (Sumner) preaches a holy crusade. But we cannot justify *war on the democratic institutions of the Southern States* as an end and object. . . . The war must be to sustain the Constitution, and prevent the establishment of an independent nation in our limits."

[1] *Advertiser*, Oct. 17, 1861.

sway of the Constitution and Laws shall be restored to all portions of our country." Thus it is clear that, though professing Union sentiments, he was not willing to acknowledge the dissolution of his own party by accepting the nomination of the Republicans. His ideal of a union party could be content with nothing short of the complete abandonment of the Republican organization; only that would satisfy either the Democratic or the Bell-Everett party.[1] Mr. Abbott did not think it necessary to give his reasons for declining, although he spoke of his nomination as being from those differing from him on political subjects. His claim to Union sentiment was in the form of a question: " How shall the government and the laws be sustained, established and maintained throughout the length and breadth of the land?"

Thus the plan for a union party failed.[2] But at bottom there was no issue between the parties; they differed only upon incidentals. The Republicans stood for Union and uncompromising support of the administration, the Democrats demanded vigorous prosecution of the war accompanied by the most liberal proffers of peace; fundamentally their aim was the same — Union. The vote, however, showed a slight increase in proportion for Andrew over the vote of 1860.[3]

[1] This was indeed the contemporary interpretation: *Journal* quoted in *Post* editorial, Oct. 18, 1861. Similarly, *Republican*, Oct. 5, 1861.

[2] After Dickinson and Abbott declined, the *Republican* commented: " The Worcester convention, so far as it undertook to be in any sense a Union convention, was unquestionably a fizzle." Oct. 18, 1861.

[3] *The vote.*

	Andrew.	Others.
1860	104,527	65,007
1861	65,261	32,062

Andrew's proportion of the total in 1860 was 62 per cent; his proportion in 1861 was 67 per cent.

CHAPTER IV

EMANCIPATION

FROM the preceding chapters it is evident that abolition was not the war-cry in Massachusetts in 1860 and 1861. The purpose of this chapter is to show that emancipation was never regarded as the main end of the war by the majority in that state, and that the Abolition movement was never universally supported; that although emancipation satisfied the anti-slavery idealism and scruples of some and was a welcome by-product to many, yet it was ever a policy of expediency for the accomplishment of the great purpose—the preservation of the Union and the perpetuation of democracy.

Since the early thirties idealists, reformers, and fanatics had championed the cause of freedom. They were few in number but great in courage; in 1831, for example, only nine persons in Massachusetts would agree to immediate emancipation; nevertheless the *Liberator* was established, and the Massachusetts Anti-slavery Society was founded the following year. In the forties a handful of people, a faction of the Abolitionists, the "Come-outers", championed the cause of freedom, and attacked the church as the bulwark of American slavery: the women took their knitting to church to show their contempt for a religion that ignored the brotherhood of men by tolerating the enslavement of some. This clique, claiming that reason and conscience were above the clergy, whom they called dumb dogs (D.D.'s), and above the Scripture, which they considered perverted by its interpretation in defense of slavery, was too extreme to gain many adherents. Another clique, including some who did not attack the religious order as a preliminary step to the freedom of the enslaved, did attack the Constitution because slaveholding politicians had construed it in favor of slavery. Yet these anti-political reformers were also too extreme to become a numerous party. Thus the thorough-going Abolitionists who saw the church, the ministry, the Bible and the United States Constitution in the way of the abolition of slavery, and who thought all must be removed, were entirely too iconoclastic to win many followers. And even in the fifties, after their early iconoclasm had failed and their aggressiveness had become more familiar and their methods less noisy and more varied, the Abolitionists still remained few in number, and were marked in their communities as queer and made the victims of mild persecution. Examples of this are not wanting. In South Hadley, Charles Eastman's barn was a station of the underground railway, and the neighbors at one time showed their contempt for him by daubing " nigger Charlie " in black paint all over his newly-painted white fence.[1] Abolitionist meetings, held in various places from time to time, were frequently occasions for disorderly conduct. In Old Hadley, for example, lads of the town threw sulphur on the stove and drove the meeting from the town hall; in West Farms, Westfield, pepper was put on the stove and the meeting was forced to adjourn to a farm-house nearby; and again in Westfield another meeting was broken up and the meeting place burned—whether set on fire purposely or by coals from the stove which had been overturned in the riot, is not known.[2]

[1] This incident was one of several told by Miss Sophia Eastman.

[2] *Liberator*, January 18, 1861. The Hadley incident was told by a contemporary, Mr. Levi Dickinson.

Yet, in spite of these demonstrations against the Abolitionists, who were regarded as cranks and fanatics, the anti-slavery cause was growing. It was strengthened by the discussions and organizations of the Free-Soil party, organized 1848, whose spirit was essentially different from that of the Abolitionists. While the latter were not a political party and would sacrifice anything, everything, even the Union itself, to be free from slavery, the Free-Soilers were a political organization who championed the cause of freedom in the territories. They worked by coalition and compromise and put anti-slavery men into prominent positions of power and leadership [1] until the Free-Soil party was finally merged into the bigger and less extreme organization, the Republican party.

The platform of the new party was clearly not abolitionist, and although it had some radical followers, the most of the extremists stood without and criticized. Yet, on the other hand, Andrew was so much too boldly anti-slavery in 1860 that the vote for him was less than for Lincoln,[2] which is but an indication of the moderate temper of the majority and their antagonism to abolition. The radical group, in the winter of 1860-1861, as earlier, remained small in number. But that number, in the words of Schouler, were " powerful in eloquence, moral in character and cultivated in intellect ";[3] their policy was aggressive; they made no compromise, sought no office, gave no quarter.

Their aggressive policy provoked hostile action from those ultra-conservative on the slavery issue; and three Abolitionist meetings, held in Boston in December, 1860, and January, 1861, were the occasions of lawless demonstrations by their opponents. A meeting in Tremont Tem-

[1] *Cf.* introduction, *supra.*
[2] *Cf. supra*, p. 33, note 1.
[3] *History of Massachusetts in the Civil War*, vol. i, p. 44.

ple, on December 3, 1860, the anniversary of John Brown's death, was invaded by a company of intolerant anti-Abolitionists, " men of respectability though not of distinction." [1] The Abolitionists and negroes were met to discuss the question, *"How shall American slavery be abolished?"* The invaders took possession of the meeting, elected their own leader chairman, and read resolutions which were adopted in the presence of the astonished regulars. [2]   The resolutions protested that

the present perilous juncture in our political affairs, in which our existence as a nation is imperilled, requires of every citizen who loves his country to come forward and express his sense of the value of the Union, alike important to the free labor of the North, the slave labor of the South, and to the interests of commerce, manufactures and agriculture of the world.

The invaders also extended sympathy to Virginia and protested against " allowing irresponsible individuals and political demagogues of every description to hold public meetings to disturb the peace and misrepresent us abroad."

[1] John Murray Forbes called them " Broadcloth rowdies." *Reminiscences*, vol. i, p. 174. Similarly Pearson, *Life of Andrew*, vol. i, p. 131. From the New York *Tribune* (Dec. 7, 1860) we learn that the mob in the afternoon was chiefly composed of merchants, traders with the South—" nearly all of whom have uncollected debts there and many of them mortgages on slaves. . . . The gentlemen sought a solace for their financial grievances by going up to Tremont Temple to trounce the handful of niggers." An evening meeting was held in a colored church in Joy Street. Robinson, Letter to the *Tribune*, December 7, names prominent participants in the mob: Rufus Choate, Jr., John Bell, B. F. Russell and Oliver Stevens of the bar; Thomas L. Parkins, a broker; Mr. Horton of the firm of Skinner & Co. (dry-goods) ; John C. Boyd, William C. Rogers, T. J. Coolidge, Jr., William Aspinwall of the old Whig state committee, and Amos A. Lawrence.

[2] *Courier*, Dec. 4, 1860; Worcester *Spy*, Dec. 4, 1860; New York *Tribune*, Dec. 5, Robinson's Letter.

The resolutions speak for themselves: they are the expression of both mercantile interest and the sincere fear that Abolitionist agitation would bring disunion and disaster—the fear of the Constitutional Unionists who foresaw in 1860 the possible disaster of all extreme positions.[1]   In connection with the mercantile interest, the anti-slavery *Spy* gave publicity to the gossip that Richard S. Fay, "the presiding genius of the riot," was a Bell-Everett man and the owner of a slave plantation in North Carolina.[2]   This may or may not have been true, but it serves our purpose: it is evidence of a conviction within the state that the extreme conservatives were associated, and even in league, with Southern interests.

It is probably true that because of trade and intercourse with various parts of the country and the world, and apart from private considerations, this mercantile class could see some factors in the situation that were unperceived by the reformers of merely local experience.   But however farsighted the invaders believed themselves to be, the whole truth as to the riot of December 3 is, that both the meeting and the invasion were mistakes.   Even Andrew, a sym-

---

[1] *Cf. supra*, p. 34, note 1.   Caleb Cushing Breckinridge Democrat of 1860, of course professed the same belief.   In a Newburyport speech he said the danger to the Union was produced by the purpose of a party at the North to act against slavery in the Southern states. The contemporary *Republican* (Feb. 29, 1860) explained: "One chief cause of the exasperation of the Southern people against the North generally arises from their mistaken notion that the radical abolitionists represent Northern sentiment . . . because those who have the ear of the South, the Southern politicians and the Northern pro-slavery presses, have an interest in keeping up the delusion. . . . But the disposition to trample on the Constitution and to disregard the rights of the Southern states is confined to a very small faction of the North, not representing a thousand of the population.   The proportion may be somewhat larger in Massachusetts."

[2] Worcester *Spy*, Dec. 4, 1860.

pathizer with John Brown, said the meeting was " injudicious and unnecessary, if not, in the present condition of the country, actually criminal." The Republican press generally condemned the calling of the meeting and sympathized with those who resolved that the record of the meeting should not go forth as the sentiment of Boston uncontradicted. The *Advertiser* even discounted the cry of free speech for those who would by their speech " embitter still further the controversy which now divides the states of this Union " ; [1] and the judicious *Republican* said the Union ought to be safe, now that a " conservative mob " had broken up the meeting of Abolitionists in Boston. Toward the rioters, however, the Republican showed its disapproval and remarked scornfully, " There are several varieties of the genus fool still extant, and there are certainly none more stupid than those who suppose they are contributing to the salvation of the Union by attempting to suppress freedom of speech in any subject." [2]   Thus it would appear that, in the state in general, commendation of the well dressed mob was in proportion to the hatred for abolition, and approval of the anniversary meeting was in proportion to belief in abolition at any price. Both factions, however, were in the minority; both were aggressive and powerful; and both continued their unwise policy.

On Sunday, December 16, 1860, Wendell Phillips spoke to Theodore Parker's church in Music Hall on *Mobs and*

---

[1] *Advertiser*, Dec. 4, 1860. It also said, as did the Springfield *Republican* and Worcester *Spy* later, that persecution was the treatment the Abolitionists thrived on.

[2] Springfield *Republican*, Dec. 4, 1860; *Sumner MSS*, from John Murray Forbes, Dec. 22, 1860: " I am glad Buchanan-Wigfall & Co. put their demands out so clearly — Suppression of free speech, free press and free labor."

Education.[1] Policemen were detailed to the meeting to prevent a repetition of the Tremont Temple affair. They were also necessary for the safe conduct of Phillips from the hall to his home, whither he was accompanied by a hostile crowd. This Sunday mob was as respectable in appearance as the mob of December 3; the cause of its assembling was also the same. It was expressed in the language of one of their members: " D—n him! he has depreciated stocks $3,000,000 by his slang."[2]

In spite of experience and wise counsel to the contrary the Abolitionists again assembled and again rioting followed. The annual session of the Massachusetts Antislavery Society was appointed to meet in Tremont Temple, January 24, 1861; its assembling was the signal for the gathering of a mob. Police protection was asked and granted, but was inadequate; the rioting was so great in the afternoon that Mayor Wightman (Democrat) had to interfere. He promised adequate protection for the evening but withdrew his promise and ordered the hall closed.[3] Again there was commendation and condemnation: for example, the *Courier* put the blame on those whose infamous

[1] *Liberator*, Dec. 21, 1860; Worcester *Spy*, Dec. 18, 1860; Sears, *Wendell Phillips*, pp. 215-216. Information concerning this episode comes from anti-slavery papers alone.

[2] Worcester *Spy*, Dec. 18, 1860. The *Spy* took delight in this quotation; for being strongly anti-slavery, it inclined to believe, with Phillips, that Boston was "choked with cotton and cankered with gold." The *Liberator* (Dec. 21, 1859) reported there were no roughs there, but "merchants' clerks," and by way of explanation — "They have to do it! It's their living! The brutal ferocity of this mob of well-dressed young men, like that of its predecessor in Tremont Temple, was incited and directed by the cotton interest."

[3] They appealed to Governor Andrew for protection, but he had no state police and could not use the militia unless so requested by the mayor. *Cf.* Pearson, *Life of Andrew*, vol. i, pp. 148-152, for full discussion. Accounts also in *Letters* of L. M. Child, pp. 147-149; *Life of Garrison*, vol. iv, pp. 4-8; *Post*, Jan. 25, 1861; and *Liberator*, Feb. 1, 1861.

teachings aim at the "overthrow of the Constitution and the destruction of the Union", while the *Advertiser* held that when the mayor closed Tremont Temple because of the threats of the mob every civil right was less secure than before;[1] but from no quarter was there defense of abolition.

From these episodes and from the comments, therefore, it would appear that Abolitionists continued to be an isolated group unapproved by the regular Republicans and attacked by Democrats and conservatives. Indeed Lowell had cautiously warned anti-slavery sympathizers, that slavery "is no longer the matter in debate and we must beware of being led off upon that side-issue. The matter now in hand is the reëstablishment of order, the reaffirmation of national unity."[2]   And though a few, like Warrington, did express antislavery ideals,[3] the majority of the

---

[1] *Courier*, Jan. 26, 1861; *Advertiser*, Jan. 26, 1861. Even the legislature was stirred. Mr. Parker, of Worcester, immediately introduced a bill to insure and protect freedom of speech, and Mr. Fisk, of Shelburn, introduced a resolution offering the Hall of Representatives to the Massachusetts Anti-slavery Society for the purpose of holding a session Friday evening. The former was sent to committee, the latter was voted down (136 to 69).

[2] Lowell, "E Pluribus Unum," *Atlantic* (Feb., 1861), vol. vii, p. 245. *Cf.* also *supra*, ch. iii, pp. 71, 76.

[3] In the *Republican*, April 20, 1861, he wrote: "I trust that slavery may go to pieces in the first shock of battle." Boutwell (*Reminiscences of Sixty Years*, vol. i, p. 262) claimed that his address to Phi Beta Kappa, June 18, 1861, called "The Conspiracy — Its Purpose and Power," was, as far as he knew, the first time that emancipation was demanded publicly, as a means of ending the war and saving the nation. Lowell, however, prophesied in "Pickens-and-Stealin's Rebellion," published in the June *Atlantic* (vol. vii, p. 763): "We cannot think that the war we are entering on can end without some radical change in the system of African slavery. Whether it be doomed to a sudden extinction, or to a gradual abolition through economical causes, this war will not leave it where it was before. As a power in the State, its reign is already over. The fiery tongues of the batteries in Charleston harbor accomplished in one day a conversion which the constancy of Garrison and the eloquence of Phillips had failed to bring about in thirty years."

Republicans were far from ready in 1861 to follow the lead
of Sumner even for military emancipation.[1] They urged,
as did the *Republican,* patience on the part of " good haters
of slavery." Nothing could be gained, they argued, by
urging abolition as a war measure upon the government,
whose duty was to suppress rebellion and " let slavery take
care of itself ! "[2]

Nevertheless the question of the status of the slaves was
raised early in national affairs by Butler and Fremont.
Butler's theory of contraband was approved as practical
military tactics.[3] The critical *Post* said: " In not returning the fugitives Butler has made no concession to Abolition, to Emancipation, to Republicanism, nor to any political question of the day. He has simply obeyed the rules
of war."[4] The *Post* even approved Fremont's order
emancipating slaves in Missouri in the same light—that of
military necessity,[5] but was satisfied with his withdrawal;

[1] *Cf. supra*, ch. iii, p. 80.

[2] Springfield *Republican*, Nov. 13, 1861, July 1, 1861. Furthermore,
on June 8 it had said: " If there is one point of honor upon which
more than another this administration will stick, it is its pledge not to
interfere with slavery in the states. As a military necessity it is among
the possibilities, though we confess that it does not look probable."

[3] Pearson, *op. cit.*, vol. i, pp. 284-285, describes the reprimand to
Butler by Andrew for offering his soldiers to Marylanders against
negro insurrection. He says Butler caught the sign of the coming
wind and for his own interest promptly veered about, and that Contraband of War was " one of the cleverest of Northern victories."

[4] *Post*, May 28, 1861. The *Liberator*, August 16, 1861, also approved.
To them it was a short step against slavery.

[5] Also the Newburyport *Herald*, Sept. 6, 1861, couldn't see the difference between Butler's decree and Fremont's proclamation. But it
wished the government would take no more account of the slaves than
of trees, and said: " The more the government gets mixed up with
the slavery question the worse it will be for all of us. The war has
nothing to do with slavery." Though as a question of military expediency the *Herald* held that the government had the power to abolish
slavery.

for it said: " It is certain now that this war is waged only
to bring back the rebellious states under the protection of
the constitution and the laws, and never has it entered into
the policy of the North to interfere with the institution of
slavery in the Southern States." [1]   In general, the Republican press merely indicated the course of the discussion,
avoiding any positive opinion,[2] although the Springfield
Republican spoke warningly:

We are to remember, what at a time like this we are prone
to forget, that we are fighting for the maintenance of the
Union, the Constitution and the laws. We have a recent law
of Congress, made to treat this particular emergency, which
defines our duty and the duty of the President to all who hold
authority from him, and to this law we must bow, if we would
hope to establish law.[3]

From two quarters, however, came pronounced opinion.
Gerrit Smith wrote to the President: " This step of General
Fremont is the first unqualifiedly and purely right one, in
regard to our colored population, which has taken place during the war." [4]   The *Pilot*, on the other hand, called Fremont's proclamation to emancipate the slaves of Missouri
a high-handed piece of violence against the Constitution of
the country, and the most criminal disregard of his instructions from Washington.[5]   On this issue, then, we find the
majority taking a moderate ground following the will of
the administration.   In the words of the *Advertiser* they

[1] *Post*, Sept. 20, 1861.

[2] This was the explanation given by the Springfield *Republican*, Sept.
21, 1861. It apparently also explains the policy of the *Advertiser*.

[3] Springfield *Republican*, Sept. 17, 1861.

[4] *Liberator*, Sept. 13, 1861.

[5] *Pilot*, Oct. 26, 1861. The *Pilot* was the Catholic newspaper of Boston, *cf. infra*, pp. 103-104.

desired "to see the government follow its own judgment
and sense of duty . . . and to see the people wise enough
to confide something to the discretion and honesty of their
chosen servants." [1]

The moderate conservative policy of standing by the administration was so widespread and the Republican party
was so unready for the emancipation issue that the anti-
slavery idealists considered a campaign of education necessary. Therefore the "Emancipation League" was formed in
Boston in December, 1861, by Dr. Samuel G. Howe,[2]
Francis W. Bird, George L. Stearns, and Frank B. Sanborn. It purposed by public addresses, by the collection of
statistics and facts, and by the circulation of valuable documents to create a public sentiment in favor of freedom.
That freedom which it urged, however, was at the beginning
not abolition, but emancipation as a military necessity, with
compensation to loyal owners, to be effective only in rebel
states.[3] For the wide dissemination of their ideas the
League established a newspaper, *The Commonwealth*, which
was edited by Moncure D. Conway and Frank B. Sanborn.

[1] Sept. 21, 1861.

[2] *Life of Garrison*, vol. iv, p. 48, note 2. The preliminary meeting
was called together at Dr. Howe's office, Sept. 5, 1861: *Journals and
Letters of Dr. S. G. Howe*, vol. ii, p. 499. Howe declared: "You cannot keep up public interest, much less public enthusiasm, about an abstraction, and Union is a mere abstraction now. . . . The word must be
emancipation."—(J. M. Forbes, *Letters and Recollections*, vol. i, p. 238,
to Forbes, Aug. 19, 1861). This was, however, no new determination
on his part; he wrote Andrew soon after the war broke out: "Since
they will have it so—in the name of God, Amen! Now let the governors and chief men of the people see to it that war shall not cease until
Emancipation is secure."—*Letters and Journals of Dr. S. G. Howe*, vol.
ii, p. 80.

[3] *Commonwealth*, Jan. 24, 1863; *Life of Garrison*, vol. iv, p. 48, note 2.
This policy was set forth by Boutwell in an address in Tremont Temple
under the auspices of the Emancipation League, Dec. 16, 1861:
Speeches Relating to the Rebellion, pp. 123-158.

But in spite of the impatient doubts of the anti-slavery factions, there were evidences that people were getting accustomed to the idea of emancipation and even admitting its wisdom, and this before the end of 1861. For, even though the unwelcome preaching of the Abolitionist had been ineffective, and though the action of the state convention in Worcester would show that the majority were far from ready for the emancipation issue, yet there had been favorable comment on Fremont's order emancipating the slaves in Missouri.[1] Moreover Amos A. Lawrence, who had been among the witnesses of one of the broadcloth riots, wrote to George Lunt, editor of the *Courier*:

The present opinion is that there should be no more compromise to sustain the union by sustaining slavery. But, on the contrary, as long as the war lasts, I believe in the propriety of the policy of confiscating the property and freeing the slaves of all active rebels wherever it can be done. And now that we must bear the hardships of war, I believe in securing the benefits of it for the advancement of freedom for the blacks and the elevating of our national character. . . . In fact, I hope that this war will not cease until a beginning shall be made of emancipation in a constitutional form.[2]

And J. D. Baldwin, editor of the *Spy*, also observed to Sumner in December:[3]

It appears to us here, as to you in Washington, that slavery is doomed. And the slavery question agitates itself so effectively now it may well be left to the progress of events. . . . The only question that remains for us, now, is this: How much is it wise for us to do to hasten or force results that are coming with such certainty? . . . Mrs. Partington trying

[1] Especially by such as the anti-slavery Worcester *Spy, e. g.,* Sept. 2 and 13, 1861; also in Springfield *Republican*, Sept. 17, 1861.

[2] *Lawrence MSS*, Nov. 9, 1861.

[3] *Sumner MSS*, Dec. 10, 1861.

to sweep back the Atlantic Ocean may be quite as sure of success as the hysterical hunkerism that now tries to avert the doom of slavery.[1]

To us, now, this seems a true observation; whether it was so in December, 1861, or whether it was the optimism of an anti-slavery champion, is rather hard to determine. Without doubt there was an encouraging tendency to consider emancipation, and in this tendency he may have foreseen the ultimate reality of which he dreamed.

The majority were becoming accustomed to the idea of emancipation; but there continued to be protests. George Morey, for example, argued that a united front was needed against the enemy, and that therefore we could not afford to bring the slavery question into Congress; for it might divide the North and lessen its power against rebellion.[2] And the *Republican,* voicing the opinion of the rank and file of its party, said: " The abolition of Slavery is not the object of his [Lincoln's] administration. He has no right to make that the purpose of the war. His present duty is to prosecute the war, and to overpower and punish the rebels who seek the destruction of the government." [3] An-

---

[1] Garrison, too, thought the anti-slavery sentiment deepening, though he regretted that " we do not come up to the standard and strike for the extirpation of the root of all our woes."—*Liberator,* Feb. 7, 1862. This was said at the annual meeting of the Anti-slavery Society which a year earlier had been the occasion of rioting.

[2] *Sumner MSS,* Dec. 8, 1861; also Springfield *Republican,* Nov. 23, 1861, and *Courier,* Aug. 20, 1861. On Dec. 13, 1861, the *Courier* said: " The House of Representatives . . . has reminded us of nothing so much as an abolition society. . . . The consequence has been that they have put in more imminent peril than before the whole cause of the Union."

[3] Dec. 5, 1861. And J. M. Forbes wrote, Aug. 27, 1861: " We must wait until the military necessity demands more positive action. When that necessity comes, the North will be reasonably united—now we are divided." Forbes, *Letters (Supplementary),* vol. i, p. 292, to David Dudley Field.

tagonists of the administration were more insistent in their condemnation, while their reasons were similar to those of the Republicans.

The winter and spring of 1862 brought forward several definite questions connected with the problem of emancipation in general. Confiscation, emancipation with compensation, emancipation in the District of Columbia, and colonization were suggested as solutions. In Massachusetts, as elsewhere, confiscation was defended and attacked: defended as a legitimate war measure for the doom of the rebels; attacked as unconstitutional, as being a bill of attainder and another way of enacting emancipation.[1] Emancipation with compensation was attacked by the extremists both radical and conservative. The *Liberator* called it " a decoy duck ", " a red herring ", " a cowardly and criminal avoidance of the one great saving issue, namely, the immediate suppression of the slave system." Garrison argued thus : if the government is acting under the war power, then any pecuniary arrangement with the rebel slave states is a sign of weakness and an act unwarranted by any power granted to it; if compensation is not warranted under the war power, then Congress has no constitutional right to vote it. It is an act of impertinence—meddling with what does not concern that body.[2] From among the other extremists the *Post* objected that Congress had no power to lay a tax on the people of the free states to pay Messrs. Carroll of Maryland for their three hundred slaves, no power to take the free labor of the North to pay slaveholders for what is property by the local law of the states.[3]

[1] Especially by Joel Parker; *e. g., The Character of the Rebellion* (pam.), pp. 33-36.

[2] *Liberator*, March 21, 1862.

[3] *Post*, April 21, 1862.

On the other hand, even conservatives such as Winthrop believed that getting rid of slavery in the border states could do no harm,[1] while administration men in general were positively enthusiastic; they called the policy of compensated emancipation " eminently sagacious " and commended the far-reaching statesmanship that had " cut the knot of the vexed question." With less enthusiasm resolutions were adopted by the legislature in support of the President's policy.[2] Emancipation in the District of Columbia was soon welcomed as "one of the greatest victories of the war." Colonization also had its active champions, for the legislature on February 28 had passed an act to incorporate the Massachusetts Colonization Society.[3]

Motley, in Vienna, as well as Charles Francis Adams [4] in England, had come to believe not only that emancipation would weaken the South and thus hasten Northern victory, but also that a clear statement of the slavery issue would prevent any alliance of the Southern states which might open the cotton ports to European trade.[5] Such an advan-

[1] *Winthrop MSS*, to John P. Kennedy, Feb. 12 and March 26, 1862; also *Post*, Feb. 14, 1862.

[2] George S. Boutwell wrote Sumner, Mar. 28, 1862: " The hunker wing of the Republicans were reluctant to approve—hesitated and then yielded." (*Sumner MSS*).

Also on April 4, 1862, resolutions were adopted approving the president's message urging gradual emancipation with pecuniary aid. *Acts and Resolves*, 1862, ch. xxxix, p. 221.

[3] *Acts and Resolves*, 1862, ch. xliv, p. 28.

[4] *Letters and Recollections* of J. M. Forbes, vol. i, p. 235. Letter of C. F. Adams to J. M. Forbes, Aug. 30, 1861: " The slave question must be settled this time once for all. . . . There is no alternative in my mind between taking it [emancipation] up and absolute submission."

[5] Holmes, *Works*, vol. xi, pp. 412, 413. Motley to Holmes, Feb. 26, 1862:

" I say, then, that one great danger comes from the chance of foreign interference. What will prevent that?

tage was perceived by some within Massachusetts; for example, the *Spy* on September 24 said: "If England or
France decides to take possession of this war against the
North, it will do it in the full knowledge that it is lending
its aid directly in support of slavery."[1] Indeed this issue
was the defense later given for the proclamation by Edward
Everett: he argued that we were gaining nothing at home
by non-interference with slavery, and were increasing the
danger of hostile intervention on the grounds that humanity demanded it and that slavery had nothing to do with
the struggle.

Thus issue succeeded issue and the people, becoming accustomed and reconciled to the idea of emancipation, were
less stirred by the attempt of Hunter to put the idea into
force than they had been by the earlier attempt of Fremont.
Its critics were strengthened in their loyalty by the President's rebuke.[2] Moreover, active workers for the Union
cause, such as John Murray Forbes, believed that through
such a policy as Hunter's the rebels could be weakened and

"Our utterly defeating the Confederates in some great conclusive
battle; or,

"Our possession of the cotton-ports and opening them to European
trade; or,

"A most unequivocal policy of slave emancipation. . . .

"The last measure is to my mind the most important. . . .

"The question is distinctly proposed to us, Shall slavery die, or the
great Republic?"

[1] Boutwell, *Speeches*, p. 193: "Now that the North . . . is put un-
equivocally on the side of freedom, it will not be easy for the British
Government to give open aid or official recognition to the rebellion."
Boutwell was among the people what the Worcester *Spy* was among
newspapers. The same view is recorded by Emerson, *Journal*, 1862, p.
442, and also published in a pamphlet, *Cheap Cotton*. Even Lydia
Maria Child said: "I am truly thankful for the proclamation. It is
doing us a great deal of good in Europe."—*Letters*, p. 171, to Mrs. L.
B. Shaw.

[2] *Post*, May 21, 1862.

the Northern armies strengthened.[1]   Indeed Warrington's
comment reveals well the anti-slavery Republican attitude:

So thought Fremont; so thinks Hunter; and so I really believe
thinks Lincoln, only his terrible habit of procrastination may
put at naught his wisdom and foresight. . . . Give him time
and he will make an end of slavery throughout the country.
. . . Yet slow as he is, he is faster than a large class of his
supporters.[2]

Barring the criticism of "procrastination", the observation
was marvelously true. Lagging critical supporters, however, continued insistently, "Let the Slavery Question
Alone." They quoted an officer in the army as saying:
"If this is a war merely for the emancipation, education
and improvement of the slaves, let us know it, and let
those fight who wish to. Our army would break up in
twenty-four hours."[3] The "merely" probably makes this
statement true, but qualified or unqualified it shows again
our thesis that abolition was not the motive of the war.
Nevertheless the soldiers in general were early in recognizing its military necessity.

[1] Forbes, *Letters (Supplementary)*, vol. i, pp. 321-322, to Gen. David
Hunter, May 23, 1862.

[2] Springfield *Republican*, May 24, 1862. Warrington in the same
article went so far as to say: "The result is sure enough. It cannot
be that the war is permitted for any other purpose than the abolition
of slavery and the reformation of American Society." This was much
farther than Republicans generally were willing to go.

[3] *Post*, June 23, Aug. 6, 1862. Also Joel Parker, *Character of the Rebellion* (pam.). Moreover the universal testimony of veterans is that
they enlisted for the defence of the Union, not for any other purpose
whatsoever; they were determined to retain the federal capital and to
maintain a road thereto, therefore their simple duty was to disperse
the rebel armies. In May, 1862, after the repudiation of Hunter, Governor Andrew said the men would not enlist unless freedom were the
purpose. This assertion was met by protest, *e. g., Post*, May 26,
Springfield *Republican*, May 30. And even Andrew forgot it when
Washington was threatened by Banks' retreat.

The marvelous growth of anti-slavery sentiment is evident when in April the *Post* quotes with approval the words of General Blair:

I am for the freedom of all races and creeds, and look for the day to come, and that not far distant, when the flag of the Union shall float over no slave, and our country shall be absolutely the land of the free; but the battle now is for the country, and the gallant men . . . give their lives for this cherished idea, and not for the emancipation of the African race.[1]

Not that the *Post* or Blair championed emancipation; for they consistently did not, but their developing anti-slavery sympathies made it possible for emancipation to be used as a war measure, even though in July the same paper said: " When treasonable abolitionism is exterminated secession will cease, the war stop and the Union be restored." [2]

The *Post*, however, was slower than individual Democrats to read the signs of the times. For example, George B. Loring of the seceders' convention in Baltimore, said in Faneuil Hall: " If the question is to be, whether the Union and the Constitution shall perish, or slavery be now abolished, if one or the other must now fall, then I say slavery must at once be exterminated, cost what it may." And this all the people applauded loud and long.[3] Even earlier than this Forbes had written to the editor of the New York *Evening Post*: " I believe to-day that the old Union Democrats, and even the true men of the border states, are ahead of Lincoln upon this question of hitting the rebels hard—with the negro or any other club." [4]   For

---

[1] *Post*, April 21, 1862.   [2] *Post*, July 18, 1862.

[3] *Post*, July 18, 1862; Springfield *Republican*, July 19, 1862, Warrington.

[4] Forbes, *Letters and Recollections*, vol. i, p. 314, to Parke Godwin, June 23, 1862.

himself he wrote Sumner: " I used to think emancipation
only another name for murder, fire and rape, but mature
reflection and considerable personal observation have since
convinced me that emancipation may, at any time, be declared without disorder." [1]   Thus by August Holmes could
write Motley:

There is a defence of blubber about the arctic creatures
through which the harpoon must be driven before the vital
parts are touched.   Perhaps the Northern sensibility is pro-
tected by some such encasing shield.   The harpoon is, I
think, at last through the blubber.   In the meanwhile I feel
no doubt in my own mind that the spirit of hostility to slavery
as the cause of this war is speedily and certainly increasing.
They were talking in the cars to-day of Fremont's speech at
the Tremont Temple last evening.   His allusions to slavery—
you know what they must have been—were received with an
applause which they would never have gained a little while
ago.   Nay, I think a miscellaneous Boston audience would
be more like to cheer any denunciation of slavery now than
almost any other sentiment.[2]

Nevertheless two days before the publication of the
Emancipation Proclamation the *Republican* had exhorted:
" Let every true man stand by the government, approve
where he can, blame where he must, but give to the men in
power the cordial sympathy and earnest support they need
and are entitled to.   If all loyal men will do this the country
is safe." [3]   There was urging of no policy, but merely of
acquiescence and loyal support.   And such was the spirit
of acceptance and conservative approval [4] with which the

---

[1] Forbes, *op. cit.*, vol. i, p. 317, to Charles Sumner, June 21, 1862.

[2] Holmes, *Works*, vol. ii, p. 167, Holmes to Motley, Aug. 29, 1862.

[3] Springfield *Republican*, Sept. 20, 1862.

[4] *E. g.*, Hampshire *Gazette* commented moderately: "A great majority of the loyal people of the North are well satisfied with this proclamation."

people of Massachusetts received the war measure. To quote again the then representative *Republican*: " Such a step can only be justified if it will save the Union." Indeed, the lack of enthusiasm for it on the part of the Abolitionists shows that even they regarded it merely as a war measure.[1]   There were, of course, a few like Asa Gray who said he did not see that the time had come for the proclamation, but who joined the general acquiescence, concluding, " I have a notion that the President knows better than I." [2]   There were, also, a few at the time who did perceive, (what it has been commonly believed all thought), that it was a magnificent deed.[3]   But the reiteration that "there is no course for genuine loyalty and patriotism but earnest and unwavering support of the government in the enforcement of the measure" shows the pervading conservative acquiescence which continued even when there was no doubt that the destruction of slavery made for the good of the country.

Yet in spite of the general assent and growing concord between men heretofore occupying extremes on public questions, there were many who claimed loyalty to the administration who regretted the steps toward emancipation. These founded a People's party to defeat Sumner, the champion of radical Abolition measures.[4]   This platform pledging support to the administration and opposing emancipation became self-contradictory on September 22; and

---

[1] Even John A. Andrew, anti-slavery enthusiast, was only moderately satisfied. He wrote Albert Brown: " It is a poor document but a mighty act; slow, somewhat halting, and wrong in delay—till January, but great and sublime after all." Pearson, *Life of Andrew*, vol. ii, p. 51.

[2] Gray, *Letters*, vol. ii, p. 94, to George Engelman, Oct. 14, 1862.

[3] *E. g.*, Emerson, *Works*, vol. xi, pp. 294-297.

[4] Full description of the platforms and election of 1862 will be found, *infra*, ch. v.

the strength of their opposition was gone, for rebellion menacing the capital still demanded support for the party of the administration regardless of emancipation. Even the *Post* almost acquiesced; its loyalty to the administration was defined as follows: " The President will be sustained in whatever he does to uphold the constitution and to subdue the rebels, but should he transcend legitimate limits— gratify the ultra spirits, he will forfeit the confidence of his fellow men." [1]   Such submission, however, was but temporary, for in January it said boldly: " The President has no authority to free the slaves *en masse*, either by constitutional law or by the war power." [2]   Yet though it was charged that the war was now a war of abolition, there still remained the consciousness that whatever the fruit of this proclamation, one duty remained to all loyal citizens —to sustain the government. Individuals also, men such as Dana, George T. Curtis, and Winthrop, who could not approve of emancipation, felt bound to abstain from injurious criticism, and so were silent. [3]

Nevertheless there were persistent critics. The *Pilot*, the Irish Catholic publication of Boston, had always been strong in its opposition to any steps toward emancipation. In 1861 it said: " Peace is impossible without the utter suppression of the Abolitionist. . . . The soldiers are not

---

[1] *Post*, Sept. 24, 1862.

[2] *Post*, Jan. 3, 1863.

[3] Dana wrote: " It *may* be right, and *may* be successful, and it has been done. Those are reasons enough for not uttering in public even misgivings about it. But I cannot give this course a hearty, intelligent support. But I can support the President."—Adams, *Dana*, vol. ii, p. 263. And Curtis in a pamphlet, *Executive Power* (p. 14), said: " This proclamation, then, by an executive decree proposes to repeal and annul valid state laws which regulate the domestic relations of their people." Similarly Winthrop, *Memoirs*, p. 228, and *MSS*, to Count Circourt, Oct. 20, and to J. P. Kennedy, Dec. 30, 1862.

in the march to abolition.   They did not enlist for anything save the vindication of the constitution."   It was largely because of the Irish antagonism to free negro labor that the *Pilot* argued for the continuance of blacks in their servile position.[1]   But late in 1863, when emancipation as a war measure was generally accepted, the Catholic editor said it should have been effected through the church alone, when she had become universal in America.   Another organ of criticism was the *Courier*.   Though this sheet was declining in power and influence, and though it was representing fewer people than in 1860, nevertheless it shows the presence of an element strongly, insistently opposed to the policy of emancipation, who ridiculed the proclamation as " a Bull against the Constitution ",[2] who then condemned it, and called to events to step backward.   For example it said: " The effect of the war on slavery has been practically nothing. . . . They must see . . . that they can have neither emancipation nor the alternative which the more desperate of them would desire—dissolution.   There is no way . . . but the old Union and the old Constitution." [3] The extreme Abolitionists here referred to were, now as always, a group of persistent critics.   That which they had demanded a year previous was accomplished, but in that year they too had gone forward; they were ahead of the general sentiment, and were demanding still more.[4]   The

---

[1] " The Irish, thank God! have too much self-respect to go for anything that will place a negro on the same grade in the labor market with themselves.   What a cause for congratulation to the poor white man is the reflection that, unlike the inferior negro race, he is at liberty to remove whithersoever his inclination may prompt him."   Quoted in the Worcester *Spy*, Nov. 22, 1862.

[2] *Courier*, Jan. 2, 1863.

[3] *Ibid.*, July 7, 1863.

[4] For example, Wendell Phillips in Cooper Institute said, in sub-

Liberator, however, generously conceded the following commendation: "Though we believe that this Proclamation is not all that the exigency of the times and the consequent duty of the government require, and therefore are not jubilant over it as many others—still, it is an important step in the right direction, and an act of immense historic consequence, and justifies the almost universal gladness of expression and warm congratulation which it is has simultaneously elicited in every part of the free states."[1]

Thus opposition, dissatisfaction, acquiescence, approval continued. At the end of the year 1863 the *Advertiser* summarized judiciously: the Emancipation Proclamation

equally disappointed its advocates and its opponents. It has failed to effect that dissolution of the rebel power which was so confidently predicted as certain to be its instantaneous effect, and has left the actual work of emancipation to be performed by the steady advance of military operations. On the other hand it has failed to make that disastrous division among the loyal which was predicted by many of its opponents. The mass of the people have acquiesced in it as a military measure taken in good faith.[2]

stance: It does not annihilate the system. In the gospel the devils came back to the swept and garnished chambers. Unless free institutions are put in the South, the old order will return in some form. Confiscate the lands and colonize them with Northern men and schools, ploughshares and seeds. Send a new government there. Organize the South anew.—*Liberator*, Jan. 30, 1863. And Lydia Maria Child lamented that it "was merely a war measure, to which we were forced by our own perils and necessities, and that no recognition of principles of justice or humanity surrounded the politic act with a halo of moral glory." (Letters, p. 171, to Mrs. S. B. Shaw.) She also said: "It excites no glow of enthusiasm, because I cannot get rid of misgivings concerning contingencies that may occur before the edict goes into effect."—*Sumner MSS*, Oct. 3, 1862.

[1] *Liberator*, Sept. 26, 1862.

[2] *Advertiser*, Dec. 31, 1863.

In the meantime various individuals of prominence had shifted their position in varying degrees.[1] Edward Everett, for example, acknowledged his stand for the Crittenden resolutions a mistaken policy and on April 9, 1863, at the inauguration of the Union Club,[2] he said: "Because we may doubt the policy of the Proclamation of the 22nd of September and 1st of January, shall we, as far as in us lies, coöperate with the oligarchy of the seceding States in forcing this 'peculiar institution' into the unoccupied territory of the Union?"[3]   Thus step by step he advanced to his unconditional support of the administration in 1864.   Amos A. Lawrence, conservative in 1860, also saw the trend of the times, but he saw it more quickly than did Everett, and worked actively with the tide; especially by aiding the enlistment of negro troops.[4]   On the other hand Robert C. Winthrop, also colleague of Everett in 1860, remained in the past.   Though he shared somewhat the growing antislavery sentiment of the time,[5] he persisted in his opposition to the majority, quietly in 1862, prominently, as Democratic elector, in 1864.   He had chosen the losing side and, though a man of gifts and prominence, was never entrusted

[1] *Cf.* chart at the end of this chapter.

[2] *Cf. infra,* ch. v.

[3] *Works,* vol. iv, p. 582.

[4] After the parade of the 54th, Amos A. Lawrence wrote in his Journal: "May God help this government to crush rebellion, and to crush its cause with it—slavery." (*Life of Amos A. Lawrence,* p. 191.)

[5] In his letter to J. P. Kennedy, April 7, 1864, Winthrop gives evidence of this: "I rejoice in your Maryland movements for getting rid of slavery in your own State, but any attempt to mend the United States Constitution at present seems to me of doubtful wisdom, to say the least.   But all's well that ends well, and if we can once more see the old Union reëstablished in peace and prosperity, nobody will be sorry that slavery may have ceased to be an element of agitation and disturbance."—*Winthrop MSS.*

with conspicuous public office, but is remembered simply as the president of the Massachusetts Historical Society.[1] A prominent conservative of the Republican party was John Murray Forbes. He had worked hard for the Union, and had championed every means for the preservation of the nation because he believed it was " the battle of democracy for all the world ", yet he described his own position as follows:

The fact is, I am not good enough to be an abolitionist, which demands a certain spirit of martyrdom, or at least self-sacrifice, and devotion to abstract principle, which I am not yet up to. I am essentially a conservative; have rather a prejudice against philanthropists, and have been anti-slavery more because Slavery is anti-republican, anti-peace, anti-material progress, anti-civilization than upon the higher and purer ground that it is wicked and unjust to the slave! I have no special love for the African any more than for the low-class Irish, but don't want to see either imposed upon. You cannot steal one man's labor or any part of it by law without threatening to steal, when you get strong enough, every man's labor, and property and life! Hence to be anti-slavery is to be conservative.[2]

These four men, with John A. Andrew, anti-slavery and

---

[1] Dr. Worthington C. Ford relates that after the war Winthrop read to the Massachusetts Historical Society a letter he had received from Everett during the war, and that with tears in his eyes he confessed his mistaken judgment in not following Everett in his support of the administration.

[2] Person, *An American Railroad Builder*, p. 109, to William Evans, an English merchant, Oct. 18, 1864. On Nov. 27, 1864, Forbes wrote to the same: " My policy would be to carry on the war, not for the abolition of slavery *eo nomine*, but for the assertion of the democratic principle, and especially for the suppression of the class which is attempting to establish an aristocratic government over the North and South." *Cf. supra*, ch. iii, pp. 76 and notes.

unionist from the beginning, and Wendell Phillips, Abolitionist *par excellence*, represent the types among the majority who acquiesced in or approved emancipation after
it was adopted as the policy of the nation.   To Phillips it
was first, to Andrew it was correlated with Union, to
Lawrence an advantageous by-product, to Forbes part of
consistent, conservative democracy, to Everett expedient,
to Winthrop perhaps all right in itself but not germane.
To the straight Democrats it was also various things:—
to the Irish an abhorrence; to the generality it came to be
tolerated; to some, such as George B. Loring, the course of
necessity and therefore of wisdom.   Thus never can it be
said that abolition was to Massachusetts the cause, the
end or the aim of the war.   There was one paramount
issue upon which all but a few fanatics were primarily and
all ultimately agreed—" the Union it must be preserved ";
Union, *not* abolition, was the watchword of Massachusetts.
Emancipation was incident and coincident; ultimately, however, it was universally accepted as a good.[1]

[1] William Lloyd Garrison at the American Anti-Slavery Anniversary,
Mar. 9, 1865, said: " Four years ago there was not a single city, town
or hamlet in the United States that would not have voted down by a
large majority the abolition enterprise.   Now there is not a single city,
village or hamlet in the land, that is loyal, that is not ready for the
immediate emancipation of those in bondage."—*Liberator*, May 19, 1865.

CHART

Illustrating the line-up of parties on emancipation 1860, and 1864-1865.

PARTIES IN 1860

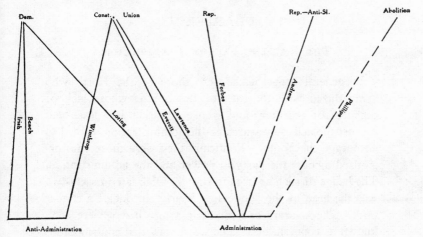

Explanation:

    The line-up of parties in 1860 shows that emancipation was not an issue.

    The men named are typical of opinions in Massachusetts.

    The slant of the lines shows the degree and direction each changed toward the policy; a line slanting to the right is advance toward and a line slanting to the left is retreat from.

    The broken line of the Abolitionists shows the weakness of their satisfaction.

CHAPTER V

THE RISE AND FALL OF COPPERHEADISM

In general copperheads were those of the North who sympathized with the men of the South; whose lack of censure for rebellion, and whose agitation for peace and against the active measures of the administration, tended to encourage the South. Politically they were those who organized against the party in power and the administration. The badge of such an organization in Ohio late in sixty-two was the head of the goddess of liberty cut out of a copper cent. The wearers and all their sympathizers were soon known as copperheads. The word was used contemporaneously in Massachusetts in 1863,[1] "hunker" having been the term used from 1860 through 1862. Popularly any criticism of any policy of the administration was dangerous, therefore copperheadism. Such a definition, however, is entirely too broad, for there were loyal supporters of the government who did not fully agree on all points, as for example on banking, or the enlistment of negro troops. On the other hand, to draw a fine line where criticism ended and copperheadism began, is at times a little difficult; for the latter term " should properly be given only to those extreme opponents of the war who went so far as to seem, by their agitation, to give aid to the South."[2] Copperheadism, therefore,

[1] Used by Charles Eliot Norton, Feb. 26, 1863, *Letters*, vol. i, p. 261; *Courier*, Mar. 13, 1863; E. W. Emerson, *Life of C. R. Lowell*, p. 255, June 7, 1863.

[2] Springfield *Republican*, March 10, 1863.

is here applied to the desire and effort to supplant the administration and to reverse its policy. Abolitionists could be included in this definition but were always distinguished as a particular kind of critic, although sometimes condemned as no better than the copperheads. Moreover the prominence of their criticism comes in the earlier stage of the war and quiets down about the time other organized opposition begins to gain strength. Their position will be kept distinct throughout the discussion.

Having followed the developing belief and growing acquiescence in emancipation from beginning to consummation, we now return to the initial stage of the war, when support of the government was impassioned and unanimous, in order to note the emergence of criticism, and to follow the rise of copperheadism through its political efforts and its fall into acquiescence and silence.

As soon as the excitement of the April crisis of 1861 was passed it was but natural that opinions should find divergent paths: some urged an aggressive policy,[1] others condemned coercive measures and commended "masterly inactivity".[2] Support of the government became less enthusiastic as the summer approached; the Abolitionists claimed that it was worse than useless to fight for anything but emancipation; and the mercantile men were feeling the disadvantage of war.[3] But the defeat at Bull Run

[1] Even as early as May 1, 1861, the Springfield *Republican* said the people were demanding that the government be more aggressive, but added, "We are confident that distrust in the government is not well founded."

[2] Especially the conservatives; for example, *Winthrop MSS*, to J. P. Kennedy, June 29, 1861.

[3] Warrington spoke of the "increasing boldness of the tory position of the democratic press" and "the commencing sensitiveness of the mercantile men."—Springfield *Republican*, June 29, 1861.

united the factions (excepting the Abolitionists) [1] again.
Newspapers, Democratic and Republican, condemned agitation for military activity and exhorted more confident
trust in the administration.[2] The majority probably realized for the first time the real magnitude of the task, and
consequently they were convinced that the prospect for anything that looked like compromise was past.[3] Indeed even
the peace faction in a Democratic meeting in Worcester
made only a " slight demonstration ", [4] and the proportional
increase in the vote for Andrew in November showed that
opposition to the administration was not formidable.[5]

Nevertheless the lesson learned in July was soon forgotten and, although the administration was supported by
the votes of the people, criticism of the moderation of the
government increased; [6] even Lowell, whose political judgment was generally very sound, expressed privately his
impatience of the President's policy, writing, sarcastically,
that " Mr. Lincoln seems to have a theory of carrying on
the war without hurting the enemy." [7] Moreover officials
of the administration were subjected to criticism, especially
Scott and Cameron; in fact, the Democrats clamored so
loud for some change [8] that it was suggested that " enemies

[1] They, of course, saw an opportunity to urge emancipation, saying
that reverses were a punishment for not freeing the slaves: *e. g.*, Sears,
Life of Phillips, p. 229: " The Government deserved to be defeated."

[2] *Courier*, Aug. 8, 1861; *Advertiser*, Aug. 20, 1861; Springfield *Republican*, July 20, 1861.

[3] Springfield *Republican* and Worcester *Spy*, July 23, 1861.

[4] Worcester *Spy*, Sept. 17, 1861.

[5] *Cf. supra*, ch. iii, p. 82, note 3.

[6] Springfield *Republican*, Oct. 9 and 25, 1861, and Worcester *Spy*, Oct.
25, 1861. Both stoutly defended inactivity, showing that the popular
demand was insistent.

[7] Scudder, *Life of Lowell*, vol. ii, p. 29.

[8] *Post*, Aug. 5, 1861; also *Courier*, Jan. 14, 1862.

(like Hunkers)" might be taking advantage of the dislike of the straight Republicans for certain members of the cabinet, and weakening the whole administration.[1] Furthermore there was an increasing lack of confidence in Lincoln: indeed, even so staunch a Republican as John D. Baldwin wrote Sumner that he was losing confidence in the executive capacity of Lincoln's administration and that doubt and discouragement were spreading among the people.[2]   The Abolitionists, of course, were most definite in their criticism; to them the President seemed incapable of generous sentiments respecting the enslaved.   They called him "a man of very small calibre" and said he had "better be at his old business of splitting rails than at the head of the government."[3]   Accordingly Wendell Phillips even declared to Sumner, "Lincoln is doing twice as much to-day to break this Union as Davis is.   We are paying thousands of lives and millions of dollars as penalty for having a timid ignorant President, all the more injurious because honest."[4]

Parallel to these noisy attacks of the fanatics was the sullen refusal of the Democrats to support the administra-

---

[1] E. g., Forbes, Letters (Supplementary), to William C. Bryant, Aug. 15, 1861. For this reason such papers as the Worcester Spy (Aug. 13) and Springfield Republican (Aug. 13) doubted the wisdom of any change.

[2] Sumner MSS, Dec. 30, 1862.

[3] Garrison MSS, to Oliver Johnson, Dec. 6, 1861.

[4] Sumner MSS, June 29, 1862. On January 9, 1862, the Republican had commented: "Most of the indirect attacks upon the government come from those who clamor for emancipation as a war measure. . . . And because they are dissatisfied on this point they seek every possible occasion for faultfinding." But Phillips' attacks on the administration became so violent that George Livermore finally wrote Sumner (MSS, Aug. 10, 1862): "Cannot you have influence with some of Wendell Phillips' friends and have him sent to a mad-house before he is arrested as a traitor? . . . If he is sane, the prison is too good for him; if crazy, have him gently treated but not suffered to go at large."

tion because they objected to confiscating the slaves of rebels and to the other related measures of 1862. Of them both the *Republican* remarked, " The fanatics and fools are still in a large majority, and the prospect is we shall do business without their help." [1] In opposition to both the administration press counselled faith in leaders, the *Republican* claiming that though " the man at the helm in this time of turmoil and danger, may be uncouth and plain of speech " yet " he is honest and wise and we shall go safely through and gain a peaceful and pleasant harbor at last.[2]

The steps toward emancipation and its final accomplishment quieted the " fanatics ". But this same progress of events increased the opposition of the conservatives until they organized to block its way. This organization was called the People's party.

Headed by " Joel Parker and Co." of Cambridge and the Constitutional Union group, and aided by J. G. Holland, (temporary editor of the Springfield *Republican*),[3] the Massachusetts People's party included the disgusted Republicans, the old-time Whigs, the moderate Democrats and a few regular Democrats. The movement was not related, as its name might imply, to the People's party in New York, for that was endorsed by the Republicans and became the Union party; but the Massachusetts movement was parallel to that of Vallandigham in Ohio.[4] The motive

---

[1] Jan. 9, 1862.

[2] April 19, 1862. This was the comment of the editor who in February, 1861, had called Lincoln " Simple Susan"; it was the exhortation of loyalty to the administration. Similarly *Advertiser* as early as Aug. 27, 1861.

[3] *Cf.* appendix ii, p, 204, note 2.

[4] Porter, *Ohio Politics during the Civil War Period*, ch. iii, pp. 138-144 (Columbia University Studies in History, Economics and Public Law, vol. xl, no. 2). Brummer, *Political History of New York State during the Period of the Civil War*, ch. iii, pp. 165-175 (Columbia University Studies in History, Economics and Public Law, xxxix, no. 2).

of the Massachusetts party, the great purpose which brought it into existence, was the defeat of Sumner, the champion of anti-slavery measures.[1]   The Hampshire *Gazette* added, " to strike a blow at the President," the *Courier* said, " to prevent the dissolution of the Union." [2]   Whatever interpretation was put upon the movement, the campaign was largely a personal one. The issue was the administration and emancipation, with Sumner and Andrew, as champions, or the administration without emancipation,—" The Union as it was "; in personality it was the administration and Sumner, or the administration without Sumner,—in short, Sumner.[3] Thus it was that the *Republican* classified the diverse elements of the party: first, Democrats who hated Sumner, because they were Democrats and in sympathy with slave-holders, and because they were men with party prejudices, party motives, etc., and Sumner stood in their way; second, hunkers, living in and about Boston [4] chiefly, who opposed him on the general principle that nobody had a right to go faster than they did, and that none but themselves had a right to hold office; third, those who believed that Massachusetts had sons who were capable of repre-

[1] *Advertiser*, Oct. 14, 1862; *Pilot*, Oct. 14, 1862; *Sumner MSS*, from Wendell Phillips, May 1, 1862.

[2] Hampshire *Gazette*, Oct. 28, 1862; also Worcester *Spy*, Oct. 30, 1862; *Courier*, Oct. 31, 1862.

[3] A meeting had been held in Charlestown as early as November, 1861, agitating his removal.—(Warrington, Springfield *Republican*, Nov. 9, 1861). In June, 1862, Andrew had warned him that hunkers would try to become the tax-collectors, and that they in their traveling from town to town might poison the minds of citizens against him and thus secure defeat through representatives sent to the legislature. (*Sumner MSS*, June 9, 1862, and *Works*, vol. vii, p. 237.)

[4] Samuel Hooper wrote Bancroft (*MSS*), Nov. 10, 1862, that the new party "embraced all the respectability and eminent gravity of Boston and its vicinity." Richard Henry Dana, Jr., and Judge Hoar both opposed Sumner. Harvard College belonged to the People's party.

senting her better than he,—men who were the truest friends to Lincoln, and who had no personal hatred, but thought somebody other than Sumner would be better for state and country.[1]   The same authority said three classes supported Sumner: first, the Abolitionists, because he represented their wild sentiments on the subject of African slavery; second, those who took him on because he was hard to get rid of or because they wanted the support of the Abolitionists; third, those who feared his defeat would be interpreted to mean that Massachusetts had changed her attitude toward slavery.[2]

The Fall campaign was opened by the Republicans.   The state convention assembled in Worcester, September 10, in response to the call for the coöperation of all " who would support the present National and State Governments, and in favor of all means necessary for the effectual suppression of the Rebellion." [3]   Its president, A. H. Bullock, argued, that in the progress of twelve months they had learned, if they did not conquer the rebellion the rebellion would conquer them, that African slavery on this continent was so intimately connected with the war that the two things could no longer be considered apart.   In this belief the convention resolved that Massachusetts, " with all her heart

[1] Oct. 20, 1862.   Earlier, Sept. 13, 1862, the *Republican* explained: " The great commercial and manufacturing interests of Massachusetts . . . do not regard themselves as completely represented in Washington by Mr. Sumner," for to him it was " the negro forever and nothing else."   Similarly the *Courier*, Oct. 7, 1862.   The Springfield *Republican*, however, preferred Sumner to a Democrat or a Boston-*Courier* Whig— either of whom would be a triumph to the rebels and an insult to the President.   J. G. Holland and his faction wanted C. F. Adams for Senator.   His *Republican* (Oct. 10, 1862) said: " If Mr. Sumner were the only anti-slavery man in the state, we would vote for him; but he is not."

[2] Springfield *Republican*, Oct. 10, 1862.

[3] *Advertiser*, Sept. 5, 1862.

and soul and mind and strength ", would support the president of the United States in the prosecution of this war " to the entire and final suppression of the rebellion ", that " the institution of slavery was the principal support of the rebellion," and that the institution " should be exterminated." [1]

On September 13, that " the loyal men in Massachusetts " might " in the most effectual manner sustain and support the government ", Joel Parker issued a call for a meeting to nominate state officers. A convention assembled October 7; it named among its vice-presidents representatives of the three parties of 1860: Josiah G. Abbott, Democrat; Edward Dickinson, Constitutional Unionist; Benjamin F. Thomas, Republican. Then the assembly adopted the congressional resolution of July, 1861, which declared that

the war is not waged on our part in any spirit of oppression, or for any purpose of conquest or subjugation, or purpose of overthrowing or interfering with the rights or established institutions of those states, but to defend and maintain the supremacy of the Constitution, and to preserve the Union with all the dignity, equality, and rights of the several states unimpaired, and as soon as these objects are accomplished war ought to cease.

They claimed to make no captious criticism of the President's acts or policy, nor to impose any conditions upon their patriotism, and they resolved " that Massachusetts with all her heart and soul, and mind, and strength, will support the President of the United States in the prosecution of this war and the entire and final suppression of the rebellion." Nevertheless they protested against the pos-

---

[1] *Advertiser*, Springfield *Republican*, Worcester *Spy*, Sept. 11, 1862, Resolutions 1 and 2.

sibilities of military despotism, desiring men in Congress
"who shall guard against the slightest encroachments upon
the legislative and judicial powers, and shall see to it
that those great safeguards to liberty, exemption from
arrest without legal warrant, trial by jury, and writ of
habeas corpus, are preserved in loyal and peaceful states." [1]

The Emancipation Proclamation of September 22 made
their position of loyalty to the President and opposition to
emancipation both ridiculous and futile. They therefore
claimed to hope that the one hundred days might change
the policy. [2] Meanwihle one vice-president rather ambigu-
ously urged "unconditional and unquestioning support of
the President in all constitutional measures, . . . in putting
down this accursed rebellion." [3] Judge Parker even said,
"I support the President, proclamation or no proclamation,
and shall continue to do so until we crush out rebellion and
restore the Union of the States. . . . Moreover," he added,
"when I see in consequence of the proclamation the flag
flying over every State from Maine to Georgia, then I
will say God bless the Proclamation." [4] Their movement
was really quashed; for the more popular abstract proposition against which they had been working was accomplished.

The Democratic convention met the day after the
People's convention and confirmed its nominations. [5] It is

[1] *Courier*, Oct. 8, 1862.

[2] Newburyport *Herald*, Oct. 20, 1862; *Post*, Oct. 9, 1862; Joel Parker,
Address to the People of Massachusetts, Oct. 30, 1862 (pam.), p. 6.

[3] *Post*, Oct. 9, 1862, J. G. Abbott's speech.

[4] *Courier*, Oct. 8, 1862, Judge Parker's speech.

[5] Colonel Devens, of Worcester, was named for governor. He had
been a Webster Whig. He was United States Marshal under Fillmore
and the first fugitive-slave case passed through his hands. He had
offered to help purchase Sims. Added to those credentials, he was a
military man and likely to get the soldier vote. Later he became a
Republican. Boutwell, *Reminiscences*, vol. i, p. 267.

interesting to note that the Democrats called to meet were those who favored " maintaining the Constitution as it is and restoring the Union as it was," expressed in the language of the congressional resolution which was embodied in the resolutions of the People's party published October 7. The Democratic resolutions, however, were more bold in their statement of opposition to the policy of the administration, for they declared: " In the name of civilized humanity, we respectfully but earnestly protest against the emancipation proclamation of the President of the United States, both on the ground of its unconstitutionality and inexpediency, and unjustifiability on the ground of military necessity." They also called upon the President to recognize the loyalty of the people by restoring to them the right of trial by jury and freedom of speech and the press.[1]   Their contention, like that of the People's party, was that the fate of the country hung on the overthrow of the radicals,[2] and in the concrete, the defeat of Sumner.

The alliance of People's Party and Democrats was doomed to failure; it rested on a mistaken judgment of the situation.   " The Constitution as it is and the Union as it was " were of the past.   Though the vote of the opposition increased from 33 per cent to 39 per cent in 1862,[3] yet that

[1] *Post*, Oct. 9, 1862. Resolutions 8 and 10 of the Democratic Convention.

[2] *E. g.*, the *Post*, Oct. 6, 1862.

[3] The graph shows this variation of political opinion very clearly; *cf.* appendix i. Moreover, the vote in comparison with that of 1861 was much larger for both parties, which showed the increased interest in the issues:

	1862		1861
Republican	80,835	....	65,261
People's	52,587	Democrat	31,266
		Scattering	796
Totals	133,422		97,323

increase was far from attaining control.   Nevertheless the opposition was growing, and it was organized.

In 1863 there was three episodes which, though not party issues, show the existence and character of copperheadism, —the visit of McClellan to Boston, the opposition to the enlistment of negro soldiers, and the draft riots.

The first episode, the visit of McClellan to Boston, was a very peaceful and rather subtle evidence of anti-admin-istration propaganda.   Though it was said that the visit was not a public affair, nevertheless public receptions were given and the *Pilot* reported that " principal merchants and bankers " closed their stores on February first in honor of the visitor.[1]   And after eight days of triumphant visiting, when, at times, thousands had waited on the street for a glimpse of this private guest, he was publicly presented with a sword by George Lunt, the copperhead editor of the *Courier*.   The sword bore the motto, " *Pro rege saepe patria semper.*" [2]

It was claimed by some of the administration men who took part in entertaining McClellan, especially by George Ticknor, that such a movement tended neither to restore him to the head of the armies, nor to make him President of the United States; it was simply a graceful tribute to his services.[3]   Nevertheless, it was generally believed by the Republican press that McClellan was invited by the old Constitutional Union group to get a popular following be-cause of military heroism and thus to lay the foundations for opposition to the administration in the presidential cam-paign of the coming year.   The Springfield *Republican* caustically remarked, that no stranger ever goes to Boston

[1] Feb. 6, 1863.

[2] *Courier*, Feb. 6, 1863.

[3] *Letters of George Ticknor*, vol. ii, p. 458, to George T. Curtis.

unless he wants something and no one is invited unless the
city wants something of him, adding, " evidently a president is wanted." [1]   The judgment of the *Spy* is in John
A. Andrew's Scrap Book, and we may therefore consider
it of value.

The Democratic party and the débris of all the parties opposed
to the administration, have not even affected to conceal that
their admiration of McClellan rose just in proportion as he
fell under the displeasure of the government.[2] They alone
applauded his delays when the government and the country
were in agony for victory. They alone were willing to receive him. . . . It wasn't that they admired him for any distinguished merit . . . but they hated the administration with
a confident and enduring hatred and found in General Mc-
Clellan a convenient instrument if he could be persuaded to
serve them. . . . The few political Brahmins deemed it a good
opportunity to concentrate all the hostile political elements in
the loyal states about a hero—and if a hero of the Peninsular
campaign is available, they will not seek for another.[3]

The furore had its run; the mass of the people tumbled
down before a popular idol; and Bullock reported to Andrew : " The work of lionizing the chieftain goes bravely on.
There is a constant buzz within the charmed circle whose
sun rises in Chelsea and sets in Back Bay." [4]   There were

[1] Feb. 9, 1863.

[2] His removal from command, 1862, had been approved by the anti-
slavery papers and disapproved by those of Democratic leanings.
(Worcester *Spy*, Nov. 11, 1862; *Commonwealth*, Nov. 5, 1862; *Courier*,
Nov. 10, 1862; Springfield *Republican*, Nov. 13, 1862.) Therefore it
would appear that the people of Massachusetts in paying tribute to a
military hero were paying tribute to one in whom they believed, contrary to the confidence of the administration, and that this movement
was, consequently, antagonistic to the administration.

[3] Worcester *Spy*, Feb. 7, 1863.

[4] Jan. 30, 1863. Similarly the Springfield *Republican*, Feb. 9, 1863.

to be sure no public demonstrations of disapproval; nevertheless the subtle leaders and the populace had to be quietly
dealt with.[1]   The course pursued is described by John
Murray Forbes in a letter to Beckwith of London:

McClellan has been starring it here in Boston, the tool of the
reactionists who hope to unite the head and sole of society,
Beacon Street and five points, Fernando Wood, Wall Street,
and Jeff Davis, the arch repudiator.   We are answering it by
forming a loyal club, pushing up Congress all we can to pass
such laws as are necessary for the rest of Abraham's reign,
by educating the people through the press.[2]

The New England Loyal Publication Society, which attempted the education of the people through the press, was
promoted by John Murray Forbes.   It, however, was not
launched against the recent demonstrations alone, for before the society was organized Forbes through his clerk
had sent out hundreds of printed slips all over the country
and through Governor Andrew to the army.   Yet, without doubt, the demonstrations of February deepened the
conviction that public opinion needed direction.   And
on March 10, 1863, John Murray Forbes, Samuel G.
Ward, Charles E. Norton and Martin Brimmer met at
Martin Brimmer's house, No. 48 Beacon Street, at 7.30
p. m., "to take steps for the formation of a society for the
publication and distribution of sound doctrine and informa-

---

[1] O. W. Holmes wrote Forbes, Feb. 5, 1863: "All the idiots, who have
been good-naturedly confounded with the imbeciles of partial intelligence, go tumbling down before the idol of the moment, in confessed
total inanity. . . . Don't let us get angry at these gratuitous exhibitions
of Punch and Judy. Let us take our tickets and look on. It is not by
attacking them that we shall gain most, but by aggressive movements
from another quarter." Forbes, *Reminiscences*, vol. ii, p. 218.

[2] *Ibid.*, vol. ii, p. 217 (Feb. 5, 1863).

tion on public affairs." [1]   Charles E. Norton and James B.
Thayer became the editors of the broadsides [2] which at the
moderate expense of $4000 were sent to individuals and
newspapers within and without the state.[3]   In many cases
the country newspapers transcribed these articles for editorials,[4] and thus consciously and unconsciously extended
the influence of the society.

The other device to meet the reactionaries, of Boston in
particular, the loyal club referred to by Forbes, was the
Union Club of Boston. All the existing clubs were lacking in staunch loyalty to the administration: the Friday
Club was composed of conservatives who, with two excep-
tions, Chief Justice Bigelow and Louis Agassiz, voted for
McClellan in 1864; [5] the Somerset Club, the largest in
Boston, was of similar sympathies. Forbes explained the
situation thus:

The fact is " club men " who live by wine and cards, tobacco
and billiards for their cheap stimulants and time killers, gravi-
tate very strongly toward secesh sympathies. They are apt to
think themselves aristocratic and gentlemenlike, and they look

[1] From MS letter in the *New England Loyal Publication Society Collection* (Boston Public Library), vol. i, p. 27.

[2] James B. Thayer edited broadsides nos. 203-218 (July 7, 1864, to
Aug.(?), 1864), while C. E. Norton was at Ashfield. Note by C. E.
Norton in the *N. E. Loyal Publication Society Collection*.

[3] According to statistics from the collection—

    August 1, 1863,   800 newspapers were supplied.

    October 1, 1863, $\begin{cases} 831 \quad " \quad " \quad " \\ 214 \text{ individuals and clubs were supplied.} \\ \overline{1045} \text{ Total.} \end{cases}$

    November 1, 1863,   1256   "

[4] Norton, *Letters*, vol. i, p. 223.

[5] *Winthrop MSS*, to Judge Clifford, Dec. 10, 1864. Agassiz was, however, according to C. E. Norton (*op. cit.*, p. 260, to G. W. Curtis, Feb.
1, 1863), a devoted admirer of McClellan.

up to the idle slave-owners with respect as being more permanently idle than themselves; at least it is so here. Hence
the public opinion influenced by our clubs is generally unsound, and there is great need of a rallying point for the unconditional loyalists.[1]

The new club had the support of Oliver Wendell Holmes,
who was optimistic in his confidence in it because, he
argued:

We shall soon find where the people stand, and when once a
rallying point is given for all who mean hearty loyalty, the
weaker brethren who do not know what they believe will walk
in with white cravats and vacuous features, and leave the
malignants in the only position they are ashamed of—that of
being in the minority.[2]

The first meeting of the new club was called for Wednesday, February 4, 1863, when McClellan was still " starring "
in Boston; it met at the house of Samuel G. Ward, No. 1
Commonwealth Avenue. Its principles, as published in the
call, were not those of any party or propaganda. They
were as follows:

1. The condition of membership, shall be unqualified loyalty
to the Government of the United States, and unwavering support of its efforts for the suppression of the Rebellion.

2. The primary object of the Association shall be to dis-
countenance and rebuke by moral and social influences, all
disloyalty to the Federal Government; and to that end the
association will use every proper means, in public and private.[3]

[1] Forbes, *Letters (Supplementary)*, vol. ii, p. 80.

[2] Forbes, *Reminiscences*, vol. ii, p. 218, Feb. 5, 1863.

[3] The call, a broadside, is among the *Lawrence MSS*. It was signed
by Edward Austin, J. Ingersoll Bowditch, John M. Forbes, James L.
Little, Samuel G. Ward, Charles E. Norton, Martin Brimmer and
Charles W. Storey. Later Amos A. Lawrence helped organize a Union
Club in Brookline and was one of the vice-presidents.

The club was finally inaugurated on April 9, with Edward Everett as president.[1] He was chosen partly because of his personal gifts, but more especially because the organizers thought it wise not to have a pronounced radical as leader, since they hoped to win members from all parties. The inaugural address is interesting for its frankness, and because it was a step toward the position that made Everett an elector in 1864, as well as because it illustrates well the position of the Union-serving conservative; he said:

I admit, however, that without being much of a partisan, I belonged to the President's opposition. But what then? There is a loyalty in opposition as well as a loyalty of support. Shall I, because I am not a political supporter of the administration, sit quietly by and see the government overturned and the country dismembered? Because we did not vote for Mr. Lincoln's administration, must we hold back from the vigorous prosecution of the war, which is to prevent Mr. Davis from installing himself at Washington? Because we may disapprove of the removal of General McClellan, shall we do what we can to paralyze the arm of his successor? Such has not been the course of McClellan himself. . . . Because we may doubt the policy of the Proclamation of the 22nd of September and 1st of January, shall we, as far as in us lies, coöperate with the oligarchy of the seceding states in forcing their " peculiar institution " into the unoccupied territory of the Union; in reopening the African slave-trade, . . . in overturning this most admirable Constitution of government? . . . Let us, then, meet it like men. Let us show ourselves equal to the duty imposed upon us, and faithful to the trust to which we are called. The cause in which we are engaged is the

[1] The officers were as follows:—President: Edward Everett. Vice-Presidents: Charles G. Loring, J. Ingersoll Bowditch, Charles B. Goodrich, William B. Rogers. Directors: Edward Austin, Martin Brimmer, George B. Chase, John M. Forbes, Samuel Johnson, Jr., James L. Little, Francis E. Parker, Harrison Ritchie. Treasurer: Samuel G. Ward. Secretary: Charles W. Storey.—Broadside in *Lawrence MSS.*

cause of the Constitution and the Law, of civilization and freedom, of man and of God. Let us engage in it with a readiness and fortitude, a courage and a zeal, a patience and a resolution, a hope and a cheer, worthy of the fathers from whom we are descended, of the country we defend, and of the privileges we inherit.[1]

The second episode of 1863 expressing opposition to the administration was the resistance to the enlistment of negro soldiers. This was shared by all parties, for it was due to race prejudice.[2] The necessity of the times, however, early convinced many: for in the winter of 1863 the demand for soldiers far exceeded the supply; it was estimated that 123,000 new men were needed annually and that in the year 1863 nearly one-half of the army was entitled to discharge and these must be replaced.[3] Later the draft impressed upon others the seriousness of the demands of the army.[4] Moreover people gradually became accustomed to the idea; for the troops, officered by the best men the state could furnish, were well disciplined and behaved well.[5] Finally the

[1] Everett, *Works*, vol. iv, pp. 581, 587.

[2] Colonel Hallowell of the 54th says: "There was a strong feeling against the negro because of his color and ignorance, and they didn't like to see him in uniform and treated as the equal of the white." Similarly the Hampshire *Gazette*, Sept. 1, 1863, and the Springfield *Republican*, June 21, said: "Not one in fifty is worth the salt junk he would eat."

[3] Springfield *Republican*, Jan. 20, 1863.

[4] *Lawrence MSS*, to Major G. L. Stearns (Nashville, Tenn.), Nov. 2, 1863; and to the Hon. Henry Nelson, Aug. 10, 1863, he wrote: "Whatever opposition existed here to the employment of colored troops has been dispelled by the enforcement of the draft. All now think alike, and those who have the welfare of the conscripts at heart are most anxious to save them from service in the extreme South and South West."

[5] It was Governor Andrew's policy to get the best officers for colored troops, especially men of real social position, for that helped remove the prejudice against the policy. The names of Shaw, Higginson and Hallowell are famous in this connection.

real situation was calmly appreciated, in the words of Amos A. Lawrence:

Our able bodied citizens are pretty nearly all in the army or navy. What we have here are not enough to do the common mechanical work. We have lost not less than 100,000 men, and some kinds of mechanical labor are at a stand. In this town where I live [Brookline] the whole number of able bodied Americans is not enough to satisfy the present call. We have enough aliens, but as long as they have work they prefer to stay here, and we cannot force them to enlist. Let us take what we can get. Negroes where well commanded make useful soldiers.[1]

Lawrence himself is an example of the shifting opinion on this subject; in 1860 he was the gubernatorial nominee of the Constitutional Unionists; in February, 1863, he said that no negroes should be encamped and drilled in the state, and if their enlistment should excite animosity it should be dropped and negroes used only for laborers;[2] in December, 1863, he said, " We need such a measure " (to fill part of our quota with negroes recruited out of the state), and finally he became active in recruiting negro troops, subscribing to the 54th and writing advertisements for money for recruiting.

For the general shifting of opinion the New England Loyal Publication Society had lent its influence. Its broadside signed "Audax " (John M. Forbes), and addressed to the editor of the *Daily Advertiser* of August twenty-fourth, presented seven reasons defending the policy:

1st. Every negro enlisted in the rebel States takes one man from the enemy's resources, and thus counts as double.

[1] *Lawrence MSS*, to J. M. Forbes, Dec. 1, 1863. Though the letter was written after the bitterness of opposition had passed, it shows well the need that quelled the opposition.

[2] *Ibid.*, to G. L. Stearns, Feb. 10, 1863.

2nd. Acclimated negroes are now admitted by even the most prejudiced to be more valuable, man for man, than unacclimated white troops at the South.

3rd. Every negro trained to arms adds to the facilities for reconstruction by taking away from the slave holders the hope of reëstablishing their peculiar institution. . . .

4th. The Emperor Napoleon . . . fully appreciated the value of black soldiers. . . . He attempted to import them into Mexico.

5th. Our friends and our enemies, in both England and France, base their hopes and their fears of our success upon our use of the negro element. . . .

6th. Economy of our home resources points to using the acclimated and unemployed blacks of the South to the greatest extent possible rather than to draw any more than we can help upon our skilled and well paid labor at the North, where every man is wanted for workshop or harvest.[1]

7th. Military service is the best mode of training the freedmen to his new duties, of preventing irregular warfare of black against white, and of raising the negro in his own self-respect and in that of his white fellow countryman.

Within twelve months, therefore, necessity, experience and education did their work: prejudice was removed and the wisdom of the policy was recognized; in fact the *Advertiser* commented, " There is probably no point as to which the progress of opinion has been more remarkable among the people of the loyal states." [2]   To the minds of the radicals, however, the departure of the first colored

[1] This was an argument of Andrew's. Pearson, *Life of Andrew*, vol. ii, p. 143.

[2] Feb. 12, 1864; also Hampshire *Gazette*, Sept. 1, 1863. The *Advertiser* itself had not advocated the enlistment of negroes in March, 1863, but on May 6th protested against the maltreatment of a negro major in Baltimore, and on November 13 advocated equal pay for the colored troops.

regiment was more than acquiescence in an administration measure of military necessity; it marked an era in the history of the enslaved race: thereby the negro would take rank among men, and be accorded a position equal to his merits;[1] the negro as a soldier became the foundation upon which to build for negro citizenship and negro suffrage.

The third episode of 1863 giving evidence of copperheadism was the draft riot of July 14. Previously (in 1862) there had been threats when a draft was impending: in fact Andrew had received from new and returned men bitter threatening letters of personal rebellion against conscription;[2] and the Society of Friends had protested against any of their number being forced to bear arms. They even held a special meeting in Boston, the thirtieth of July 1863, to call attention to their ancient discipline that they were not to enlist even when drafted, nor pay the commutation.[3] Such murmurings were to be expected, but the riot of July was a crisis which at the time seemed portentous.

The immediate cause was the serving of notices on drafted men of the North End. When David Howe, who was performing his duty, called at a house in Prince Street, he was attacked by the drafted man and his friends. Howe was badly injured; a mob gathered and attacked the police; but arrests were made and squads of police were stationed in different parts of the North End to prevent a spread of the tumult. The military were ordered to their respective armories, and at five in the afternoon the third company of heavy artillery arrived from Fort Independence. Never-

---

[1] Worcester *Spy*, May 29, 1862, and Hampshire *Gazette*, Sept. 1, 1863.

[2] *Andrew MSS*, July 8 and Aug. 6, 1862, and July 4 and Aug. 18, 1863.

[3] From a Broadside calling a meeting. Also *Andrew MSS*, from the Society of Friends, Sept. 9. 1862.

theless in the early evening, at seven o'clock, a large and boisterous crowd assembled in front of the Light Artillery Armory in Cooper Street. The windows were smashed and missiles fell about the men within. Finally when the door was broken in, Captain Jones ordered the man at the gun to fire. Several fell and the rabble dispersed; the killed and wounded were dragged away, unnumbered and unnamed. Another exciting scene occurred in Dock Square: there hardware stores were robbed and the crowd armed itself with rifles, pistols and bowie knives. Again regulars from Fort Independence arrived; the square was cleared by the police and strong guards were placed along the streets; pieces of cannon of the first and second companies of the heavy artillery were placed so as to sweep the square; and a military patrol was established for the rest of the night.[1]

Thus the *Advertiser* was able to conclude its account as follows:

As we go to press the military are at their posts and all is quiet. Little knots of people, however, still linger about Cooper and the adjacent streets but threaten nothing serious. It is gratifying . . . to record the complete triumph of law and order in the fearful scenes of yesterday and the unhesitating and stern display of military power to accomplish that end.

The editors should have been gratified also because of the forehandedness of their efficient governor, who, learning from the police that there was a mob of 5000 at the North End, immediately ordered Major Gordon to send whatever of the 11th Infantry he had at the Fort. The Governor's own comment was: " I began my work the moment I arrived in Boston, thinking the New York movement was sympto-

---

[1] New York *Tribune*, July 15 and 17, 1863; *Advertiser*, July 15, 1863; Pearson, *op. cit.*, vol. ii, pp. 133, 134

matic of a wider disease, and I was three hours ahead of
the mob, so that we had troops ready to turn over to the
municipal authorities before there was any real outbreak." [1]

In all probability the riot had gained some encourage-
ment from New York, for "any phase of popular excitement is liable to go over the country like a wave ".[2]   The
public mind was excited; meetings had been held Monday
night (July 13), and some intemperate and treasonable
speech had been indulged in.   The rabble of Tuesday, however, was so quickly and forcibly dispersed that there was
no outbreak elsewhere.   Moreover the majority of Massachusetts citizens saw beyond personal interest and believed
the draft a wise policy, for it showed the vigor of the
government at the same time that it would furnish men
needed for victory.   These, the great law-abiding classes,
believed if the government had ordered it, the demand
must be met.[3]   Every paper except the *Courier* [4] held that
" the laws must be sustained; the peace preserved, else the
government becomes a mockery and existence worthless." [5]
The excitement, accordingly, soon died down, and by July
25 the *Spy* commented:

Whatever hostile political influences may have been concerned in these riots, whatever conspiracies may have sought

---

[1] *Andrew MSS.*   [2] Contemporary view of the *Journal*, July 15, 1863.

[3] Especially, Springfield *Republican*, Aug. 5, 1862; *Advertiser*, July 8
and 31, 1863; and *Post*, Mar. 11, 1863.

[4] The *Courier*, July 14, 1863, said of the New York riot: "If this
Government undertakes to set itself above the fundamental law of the
land on whatever pretext, the populace will feel itself freed from obligations of law, otherwise held sacred, whenever the provocation to do
so occurs.   When this state of things comes about, anarchy is begun.
. . . Those, therefore, who have advocated the setting aside of the constitution, upon the plea of military necessity, may see plainly the conse-
quences."

[5] These were the words of the *Post*, July 16, 1863.

this method of doing injury to the government, they never for one moment deserved the consideration that has been given to them. . . . Here and there anonymous and unknown writers in copperhead newspapers express a kind of cowardly sympathy for the scoundrels, and seek to keep alive the false impression of wide-spread disaffection and hostility to the measures of the government.

Later on, in 1864, there are indications of some fear of more riots but no outbreak occurred.[1]

Thus if we to-day should pass judgment on the manifestations of copperheadism in 1863, it would appear that the visit of McClellan was evidence of the most serious opposition to the government, for the political organization that finally nominated him gained steadily in strength and influence, while the riots were permanently quelled and negro troops became an established institution. The political register for the year gives no evidence of any formidable opposition to the administration. Since this was an off year the election was naturally less important than a senatorial or presidential contest and consequently fewer votes were cast. But it is interesting to note that the loss was in anti-administration votes; opposition to special issues evidently did not mean opposition to the administration; moreover no campaign could prove that the President was inefficient. The votes cast were as follows:

	1863	1862	1861
Republican	70,483	80,835	65,261
Democrat	29,207	52,587	31,266
Scattering	77	......	796
Republican majority	41,199	28,248	33,199
Totals	99,767	133,422	97,323

[1] *Andrew MSS.* John A. Andrew protested to Gen. J. A. Dix, commanding Department of the East, against the removal of Cabot's Heavy Artillery—one reason given was the danger of riot in Boston and the

Turning these into percentages we note that the Democratic vote had fallen to 29 per cent in comparison with 39 per cent in 1862 and 33 per cent in 1861.[1]

The campaign is interesting because the issues of the future become apparent. The principal planks of the platforms, however, referred to the issues of the current year. The Republican platform, for example, pledged " unwavering and unconditional support to the national government "; it spoke of the contest " between slavery and liberty ", and approved the Emancipation Proclamation as a measure of military necessity and " as a guaranty to the world that the contest is for civilization and Christianity." This position was a great advance on that of 1860. It was then held by a few; in 1863 it had the support of the majority. The Republican platform also expressed confidence that no rights nor personal freedom would be destroyed; it deprecated the idea that permanent peace could be built up while slavery existed; Republicans would therefore treat as enemies those who would make peace with rebels on any terms short of submission to national authority and the suppression of their pretended confederacy. To that end they approved the use of colored soldiers on the basis of perfect equality as to rights and compensations.[2]

The Democrats, in turn, were no less bold: " The Government sustained but the administration censured " were the head lines in the *Post*.   Judge Abbott said they were to inaugurate " a movement . . . to bring together and unite all the opposition to the unconstitutional acts of the party in power " which should result a year hence in sweeping that party into oblivion.[3]   To that end they said it was " the

surrounding cities in case of a draft, April 22, 1864. He also ordered Lieutenant-Colonel Holmes to hold himself " ready for street work in case of a draft."

[1] *Cf.* graph, appendix i.   [2] *Advertiser*, Sept. 25, 1863.

[3] *Post*, Sept. 4, 1863.

duty of every citizen to sustain the National Government ";
they also stated that the paramount objects of the Democracy were " to restore the union as it was, and to maintain
and abide by the Federal Constitution." Therefore they
were opposed to the doctrine of secession, to all interference
on the part of the National Government with local and domestic affairs in the several States, to the exercise of any
implied powers by any department of government, to efforts to continue the civil war for purposes of subjugation
or emancipation, and to the extension of martial law over
states not in rebellion.   They also argued, and thus introduced the issues of the future:

that as our Union is composed of independent sovereign
states, no one of which has yet been wrested from the Union
by force of arms, we look with abhorrence on the proposition
of leading Republicans to thrust any state out of the Union,
under pretense that by the rebellion of any part, or the whole
of the citizens of any State, such State has ceased to form
an integral part of the Union. That whenever any state shall
lay down its arms and submit to the laws and the constituted
authorities, the people thereof be entitled to resume and enjoy
all the rights and privileges given by the laws and Constitution
to the citizens of the several states.[1]

Dr. Loring, in particular, laid stress on the new issue; ad-
dressing the convention he said the Democrats had wanted
to go into this campaign with the declaration that

when a sovereign state which has withdrawn from this Union,
whether by Convention or by sending her Representatives to
Congress again shall determine to return to it, the doors shall
be thrown open and she shall be welcomed back once more.
. . . You may feel wronged at the outrages the Administration has committed, but those are things that pass away as the

---

[1] *Post*, Sept. 4, 1863; *Courier*, Sept. 4, 1863.

administration goes on, as mud thrown from the wheels, but there remains that great principle without which Massachusetts is not safe, and Maine is not safe, and that is that they are still free and independent states under the Constitution.[1]

This primary Democratic doctrine of state rights, however, was not the issue of the day. Neither was the detailed attack upon the administration policy to succeed, for men such as Richard Henry Dana, Jr., who opposed Sumner and his theories, stood by the administration; in fact in his Cambridge speech of October 5 Dana said:

The questions and means and final settlements, and the doctrines on which they rest, should be matters of reflection and study,—to some extent public discussion, but not made in advance conditions of loyal coöperation. . . . While the war lasts, let us have, if it be possible, one heart, one voice, and one hand.[2]

Thus the issue in 1863 was the preservation of the Union by the policy of the administration. The will of the people sustained it.

The next issue, that of 1864, was peace—by compromise under a new administration or by military success under the present régime.

To be sure peace men had existed from the beginning: in the winter of 1861 they had been insistent on participation in the Virginia Peace Conference, and as soon as the outburst of passion which followed the firing upon Sumter and the attack upon the Sixth had subsided, the demand for compromise could be heard from time to time until in December, 1862, Ralph Waldo Emerson, writing to Thomas Carlyle, conditioned his hopes thus: " If we can stave off the

[1] *Post*, Sept. 4, 1863.
[2] *Advertiser*, Oct. 6, 1863.

fury of trade which makes peace at the cost of replacing the South in the *status quo ante bellum.*" [1] The following month (January, 1863), the editor of the Boston *Journal* thought things looked gloomy and spoke of "the peace schemes of the Northern traitors and submissionists"; and in the summer of the same year even the conservative Newburyport *Herald* took occasion to exhort men to support the government, making the best of what was unavoidable. [2] The New England Loyal Publication Society had perceived that the tendency to make any possible peace was at work. It issued broadsides written by Charles Eliot Norton: one to show that the "Peace-at-any-price men" encouraged the rebels in the belief that their course was not utterly hopeless and thus were lengthening the war; [3] the other argued that any peace would be a confession of national defeat. For the national authorities had no power to treat with the rebels, who had no character which could enable them to become parties to a treaty of peace. In brief he said, "We have nothing to ask, the rebels nothing to give but submission." [4]

But in spite of all argument the demands for peace and criticisms of Lincoln grew louder and louder. Drafting, repeated military defeats, heavy taxes and high prices, all increased the general desire for a respite. This desire became formidable in 1864. There were "Political Peace Putterings at Niagara Falls", and finally the Democrats in Massachusetts resolved that "justice, humanity, liberty and public welfare, demand that immediate efforts be made

[1] *Correspondence*, vol. ii, p. 281.

[2] June 13, 1863.

[3] Broadside no. 71 (May 29, 1863). The same argument was published in the *Advertiser* on August 22, 1864; also *Bancroft MSS*, John Murray Forbes to George Bancroft, Sept. 7, 1864.

[4] Broadside, no. 66.

for a cessation of hostilities.[1]   When the national platform
was ratified in Faneuil Hall, the Hon. J. G. Abbott made
an appeal to the motive of personal comfort.   " The reëlection of Lincoln ", he declared,

means war for the next four years. It means drafts, drafts,
drafts till there is nothing more to be drawn. It means debt
that is threatening us every day with national bankruptcy. It
means starvation prices. It means grinding and vexatious
taxation, so that a man, from the time he is born into the
world can do nothing—can't get married and can't even die
—without being taxed.[2]

The meeting accordingly resolved that the administration
of Lincoln had failed, and that the great purpose of the
Democracy would be to restore and maintain the Union, to
reëstablish the Constitution and the laws and to obtain an
honorable peace. On September 21 the state convention
passed bold resolutions claiming that the only chance for
the securing of an honorable peace " was by expelling from
power the present corrupt, imbecile and revolutionary administration " and returning " to the policy to which the
Executive, Congress, and the People were solemnly pledged
in the Crittenden resolutions, coöperative movements toward Peace and Union." [3]

Unquestionably the popular will was then truly set forth
by Amos A. Lawrence; to Robert M. Mason he wrote:

[1] Springfield *Republican*, Aug. 31, 1864.

[2] Sept. 17, 1864; *Post* (supplement), Sept. 19, 1864.

[3] *Post*, Sept. 22, 1864. The nominees for electors-at-large were chosen,
Robert C. Winthrop and Erasmus Beach. The latter, the Democratic
nominee for governor in 1860, is an example of the persistent Democrat, while Robert C. Winthrop is representative of the conservative
who failed to perceive the trend of the times. *Cf. supra*, ch. iv, p. 106
and chart, *supra*, p. 109.

From present appearances we must have peace before many months, either by the defeat of the rebel armies, or by the will of the people of both sections; for there is no doubt that the people, the working men and women, want peace: and the government cannot long refuse to reflect the will of the people.[1]

There is, in fact, no doubt that discouragement because of lack of success in battle, criticism of the Executive, and the desire for personal comfort, were all adding many to the Democratic ranks. It could scarcely be otherwise when even loyal Republicans such as Forbes and Andrew had questioned the wisdom of the administration.[2] They, however, were confident of Lincoln's popularity with the people. And, in truth, this confidence was merited; for, when victories in the field came to lessen the discouragement, the people did hope for peace without compromise,[3] and did support the administration loyally.

In the meanwhile notwithstanding discouragement and questionings the Republicans, in convention on September 15, answered with assurance the increasing demands for peace. They enunciated again the duty of every citizen " to maintain the integrity of the Union, the supremacy of the National Government and the paramount authority of the national constitution "; they upheld the " acts and proclamations by which the government, in self-defense, and in wise zeal to save the Union, has sought to destroy slavery and make the nation all free "; they sustained " the National Government in its determination not to recognize the Confederate rebel leaders as a political power ", and

[1] *Lawrence MSS*, Sept. 4, 1864.

[2] Forbes, *Letters and Recollections*, vol. ii, p. 89 (April 28 [1864]), and Pearson, *Life of Andrew*, vol. ii, p. 162.

[3] *Ibid.*, Sept. 13, 1864.

called upon the national administration to maintain their position that " no compromise can be made with rebels that is not based upon their unconditional surrender to the authority of the National Government and their return to allegiance to the Constitution and the laws of the United States." [1]

With this platform the Republicans, or better the party of the administration, gained allies from various quarters. For example the vice-presidents of the ratification meeting of September 28 included Josiah Quincy, Amos A. Lawrence—Union men, and Oliver Wendell Holmes, Martin Brimmer, J. Ingersoll Bowditch and Henry I. Bowditch, of the anti-slavery group. Moreover the Abolitionists openly joined the Republicans, whose platform was now sufficiently outspoken in its anti-slavery demands to satisfy even those who had aided in the nomination of Fremont at Cleveland. Indeed Garrison regretted that Phillips would not alter his opposition to Lincoln.[2] As always Phillips had a few followers, but the rank and file supported Lincoln. Lydia Maria Child undoubtedly voiced their position when she said:

I suppose, taking all things into consideration, we can have no better president than " honest Abe ", with his slow mind and legal conscience forever pottering about details and calculating chances. I believe he deserves the universally conceded epithet of " honest ", and I think he sincerely wishes to have Slavery swept completely away. But he obviously lacks sympathy for the wrongs and sufferings of the colored race; and, religious-minded as he seems to be, his fear of God is unfortunately secondary to his fear of the Democratic Party.

[1] *Advertiser*, Sept. 16, 1864.

[2] *Garrison MSS*, to Samuel May, Jr., 1864. *The Anti-slavery Standard* and the *Liberator* both supported Lincoln.

Still, I wish him to be reëlected. . . . As for Fremont I have long feared that he was a selfish, unprincipled adventurer.[1]

In the end Lincoln was elected because the people believed in him;[2] his election was their voice, not that of the politicians. After his nomination the *Republican* had explained at length:

The people believe that Mr. Lincoln is honest, that he deals with all public questions on their merits, that he has no purely selfish ends to serve, that he is in earnest, that he is no rider of mere hobbies, that he believes in the people and tries to execute their will, that his morals are pure, that he is in the hands of no man and no cabal, and that he has in him the power to reconcile more jarring interests and antagonistic wills than any other man. . . . The people have identified Mr. Lincoln with the financial welfare of the country. . . . The present standing of the national credit rests upon the policy of crushing the military power of the rebellion, and putting it beyond the voice of its leaders to dictate settlement. The money power is greater at this time than it has ever been before— greater and more widely diffused among the people. The government money is in every man's hand and government bonds are universally held by the thrifty people of the country. It is beyond dispute that the money power of the country is pleased with this selection.[3]

Lowell was right when he observed, " The mercantile classes are longing for peace, but I believe the people are more firm than ever." [4]

[1] *Sumner MSS*, July 31, 1864.

[2] *Ibid.*, from C. E. Norton, April 29, 1864: " Lincoln's popularity is very great, far greater with the mass of the people than some of our politicians seem to suppose." This is likewise the testimony of F. B. Sanborn and the contemporary comment of the *Advertiser*, June 9, 1864.

[3] June 13, 1864.

[4] *Letters*, vol. i, p. 336, to J. L. Motley, July 28, 1864.

The strength of McClellan had been lessened appreciably by his letter of acceptance. It was, of course, extravagantly praised by the partisan papers supporting him.[1] Nevertheless the soldiers, with whom he was personally popular, felt that although it was patriotic and would have suited if he had refused the nomination, yet when he concluded by saying he thought his views expressed those of the convention, he changed "from a big honest straightforward soldier, into a politician seeking office."[2] Although a McClellan meeting, in Boston, proclaimed that the general's merit was that of the founders of the government, "conciliation and compromise,"[3] this did not suffice. Men had in fact come to believe that circumstances had changed and that what was at first a struggle to maintain the outward form of our government, had become a contest to preserve the life and assert the supreme will of the nation; that it was not against the constitution alone that the rebels declared war, but against free institutions. This John Murray Forbes evidently had in mind when he wrote F. P. Blair:

Mr. Lincoln must not depend upon the rich and aristocratic classes, nor upon the city people; he must appeal to the hard-handed people of the country, upon a plain, square issue, which they can understand. . . . On the other side, the aristocratic party have an immense bribe held out to them in the control of the government for four years, and the opportunity it would give them to change our form of government into a permanent oligarchy.[4]

[1] *Courier*, Sept. 10, 1864; *Post*, Sept. 10, 1864.

[2] C. F. Morse, *Letters*, p. 191; also the testimony of Dr. Samuel A. Green, who was then in the army.

[3] *Courier*, Nov. 7, 1864.

[4] Forbes, *Letters (Supplementary)*, vol. ii, p. 288, Sept. 18, 1864. C. E.

Similarly Edward Everett said: " We are now called upon to overthrow the administration, and restore the Democracy, in the vain hope of bringing the men who, for selfish and ambitious purposes, have waged the war back to the Union which they tell us they loathe, by new guarantees and further compromises." [1]

The issue was really union, not the Union as it was but a new union, which could be realized not by peace through compromise but by peace through the policy of the administration. Declarations such as that of Jefferson Davis quoted by Edward Everett, " We are not fighting for slavery, we are fighting for independence, and that or extermination we will have ",[2] convinced some; but military victory encouraged the people generally, and the administration was sustained by a strong majority. They gave 126,742 votes to Lincoln and only a third as many or 48,745 to McClellan. The opposition had been bolder and more outspoken than ever. McClellan had even carried some towns, but the proportion of the total vote for the anti-administration party was smaller than ever; this year it was (in round numbers) but 28 per cent in comparison to 33 per cent, 39 per cent and 29 per cent in 1861, 1862, and 1863 respectively.[3]

When the result was known Governor Andrew com-

Norton had the same idea; he wrote G. W. Curtis on June 24, 1864: " The war is a struggle of anti-democrats with the democrats; of the maintenance of the privilege of a class with the maintenance of the common rights of man." *Ibid.*, vol. i, p. 269.

[1] Everett, *Works*, vol. iv, p. 724. He added: " They have decided the course which I have felt it my duty to take." In 1862 he had described his political position to George Bancroft, calling it "unsatisfactory neutrality." (*Bancroft MSS*, Oct. 27, 1862.)

[2] *Advertiser*, Oct. 20, 1864. Everett to the Union meeting, Charles G. Loring presiding, Faneuil Hall, Oct. 19.

[3] *Cf.* graph, appendix i.

mented, " We have knocked down and stamped out the last
Copperhead ghost in Massachusetts." [1]   And this was apparently true; for when the election was over the friends
of the general (with the exception of the *Courier*) acquiesced in the decision and determined " to settle down
to the ordinary pursuits of life, giving the administration
for the next four years all the support it can ask for in its
endeavors for the integrity of the constitution, the preservation of the Union, and the restoration of peace in the land." [2]
Such passive acquiescence continued to be the general attitude [3] from the election to the assassination; in fact active
opposition had failed by the will of the people, and events
moving rapidly in the field tended to restore confidence.
Though not all were enthusiastic in their praise of the
message to Congress in December, there had been no violent
criticism; and finally on February 13, 1865, even the Democratic *Post* gave up the peace plank it had so fervently advocated four months before. It admitted: " The tone of the
Rebel press and of Mr. Davis's speech at Richmond, now
is as fierce and uncompromising as it ever was; and there is
a renewal of the old vows as to dying a thousand deaths
rather than give up the independence of the confederacy." [4]
It is thus very evident that time and circumstance had weakened copperheadism.

[1] Pearson, *op. cit.*, vol. ii, p. 176. Emerson also said: " The people
have this autumn expressed their decision that the nation shall be a
nation."

[2] *Pilot*, Nov. 12, 1864; also *Post*, Nov. 9, 1864.

[3] There was, however, from time to time moderate criticism even by
friends of the administration. *E. g.*, Andrew wrote Forbes in the
winter of 1865: " I think that the administration lacks coherence,
method, purpose, and consistency; not in the sense which impugns its
patriotism, or its philanthropic will either, but in a sense which affects
its intelligent unity of purpose." Forbes, *Recollectons*, vol. ii, p. 122.

[4] *Post*, Feb. 13, 1865.

The assassination of Lincoln removed every trace of it. All factions forgot their differences and, as at the firing on Fort Sumter, there was again a united people; real patriotism was not lacking in the hour of need. Each faction seemed to outdo every other in appreciation of the great man. Remembering that the Abolitionists had called him " a man of very small calibre ",[1] it is interesting to read the *Liberator* :[2]

No President in our day had so thoroughly, or in so large and wise a sense identified himself with the people, sought to strengthen and build up the powers of the people, sought to give expression in his official acts to their deliberate purpose and known will, and to develop their best interests, as Abraham Lincoln. The people everywhere understood him, and felt sure of him. They felt that he was thinking, planning and working, with a sincere desire to promote the high and noble ends for which the republic was created, and they had given him their confidence, their respect, aye, and their love, as to no predecessor whom they have ever known.

Even the *Post*, while enumerating his simple good qualities, faithfulness, honesty and patriotism, conceded, " He must have possessed a superior faculty for moulding and ruling men "; they also transformed what to some had been faults into probable virtues, saying, " It is probable that much of his success as the Executive Head of the Nation resulted from his apparent easiness of disposition.[3]

Of course such men as Andrew immediately forgot their minor differences with the administration, and praised the ruler than whom in all human history there was none " more just, unselfish or unresentful." [4]   And such men as

---

[1] *Cf. supra*, p. 113.   [2] April 21, 1865.

[3] May 4, 1865.

[4] Pearson, *op. cit.*, vol. ii, p. 245, note 2.

Edward Everett Hale were willing to acknowledge their previous misjudgment; Hale, in fact, wrote Charles Sumner: " I feel as if I ought to apologize to you personally for hard things I have said of Mr. Lincoln to you when you must have known so well what he was and what he was doing." [1] And finally even Robert C. Winthrop, who had remained determinedly anti-Republican, wrote his friend J. P. Kennedy: " I have no words to express my horror, and my real grief for the death of the President. He had won upon me greatly during the last few months and I had begun to like him." [2] Moreover this last prominent representative of the old " Cotton Whigs " gave the following eulogy:

The cheerful courage, the shrewd sagacity, the earnest zeal, the imperturbable good-nature, the untiring fidelity to duty, the ardent devotion to the Union, the firm reliance upon God, which he has displayed during his whole administration; and the eminent moderation and magnanimity, both toward political opponents and public enemies, which he has manifested since his recent and triumphal reëlection, have won for him a measure of regard, of respect, and of affection, such as no other man of our age has ever enjoyed.[3]

Among the common people there was deep, sincere grief. If perchance here and there individuals were not likewise sorrowful those individuals expressed publicly their allegiance or left the neighborhood.[4] Thus in the national

[1] *Sumner MSS*, May 1, 1865.

[2] *Winthrop MSS*, April 21, 1865.

[3] Winthrop, *Speeches*, vol. ii, p. 662, before the Massachusetts Historical Society, April 20, 1865.

[4] One man, for instance, was tarred and feathered and compelled to carry the Stars-and-Stripes through the streets of Swampscott. Finally, having cheered the flag, he was allowed to go home on condition of keeping the flag at half-mast for thirty days. At Fall River the

disaster every vestige of copperheadism was lost, and a united people were ready to support the new president and undertake the new problems.

people compelled a liquor dealer to do the same. (*Life of Bowditch,* vol. ii, p. 50.) In Danvers a crowd gathered at Goodale's shoe factory. Goodale had had a political altercation with some neighbors, and on reaching his office had refused to allow the factory girls to replace at his window the flag, which they had bound with crape. The mob with the pot of tar insisted, and moreover he saluted that flag. (Told by Miss Harriet Goodale.)

PART I

CHAPTER VI

RECONSTRUCTION—THEORIES AND POLICIES

PROFESSOR DUNNING, in his *Essays on the Civil War and Reconstruction*, analyzes the theories bearing upon reconstruction that became prominent in Congress after 1863.[1] He distinguishes five, which may be grouped thus: first, those recognizing the existence of the state which had attempted secession,—the Southern and Presidential theories; second, those denying the existence of the state,—Sumner's state suicide and Stevens' conquered province theories; and third, the forfeited rights theory of Congressional reconstruction.

It might be natural to suppose, from the fact that Massachusetts supported Congressional reconstruction in the elections of the late sixties, that Sumner's theory was the will of Massachusetts or that it was immediately accepted by the people of the state; but such was not the case. If he was ahead of his party when he advocated emancipation in the state convention of 1861, he was at variance with it when he declared that secession sustained by force " becomes a practical abdication by the state of all rights under the constitution, while the treason it involves works instant forfeiture of all functions and powers essential to the continued existence of the State as a body politic ", and therefore Congress should "assume complete jurisdiction of such vacated territory " and should proceed to establish therein

[1] Pp. 99 *et seq.*

republican forms of government.[1]   He argued, of course,
that slavery, a local institution without origin in the Constitution or in natural right, had ceased to exist when the
state ceased to exist.   It is evident that his reconstruction
theory was but a means to the realization of his all-absorbing
ideal, but it is very clear that his ideal was not the goal for
which the people of Massachusetts were fighting;[2] moreover his method was totally at variance with all their rea-
soning.   In fact Republican as well as Democrat—*Advertiser* and *Courier*, Hampshire *Gazette* and Newburyport
Herald—all argued with the Springfield *Republican* and the
Boston *Post* that "the Constitution of the United States
does not recognize secession as a legal act in any way; therefore the state is not out of the Union".   The Northern
states were at war to convince the states of the Confederacy
that they could not legally withdraw; if the North accepted the position of Sumner it conceded to the rebels
all that they asked, namely, the right of secession; and to
conquer the Southern states conceding the very principle
for which these men were contending, would involve a
gross inconsistency.[3]

The Democrats, however, made the constitutional basis
of the Union an issue, resolving in 1863, "That as
our Union is composed of independent sovereign states, no

[1] *Cong. Globe*, 37 cong., 2 sess., pt. i, pp. 736-737 (Feb. 11, 1862);
Sumner, *Works*, vol. vi, pp. 301-305; Pierce, *Sumner*, vol. iv, p. 73.

[2] *Cf. supra*, ch. iii.

[3] Springfield *Republican*, Feb. 25, March 21, June 18, 1862; likewise
Courier, Mar. 3, 1862, *Pilot*, Sept. 17, 1864, *Post*, May 22, 1862, Aug. 25,
1863, June 1, 1864; also various pamphlets: William B. Greene, *Sov-
ereignty of the People*, pp. 23-24; and Joel Parker, *Status of the South-
ern States*, p. 59, *Revolution and Reconstruction*, pp. 39, 61, 64, and
*Constitutional Law with Reference to the Present Condition of the
United States*, pp. 23-27.   The last was also printed in *North American
Review*, April, 1862.

one of which has yet been wrested from the Union by force of arms, we look with abhorrence on the proposition to thrust any state out of the Union under pretence that by the rebellion of any part of the citizens of any state, such state has ceased to form an integral part of the Union." Therefore, since the paramount object of Democracy was to restore the Union as it was, they condemned the effort on the part of the administration " to continue the present deplorable civil war for the purposes of subjugation or emancipation." [1]

The Republicans, notwithstanding, refused to take issue. Even in 1865 they held to their war theory concerning the relation of the states to the Union. For example, on January 24 the Hampshire *Gazette* said:

When the rebellion ceases, those states will be as much members of the Union, as they ever were, and when they acknowledge their allegiance to the general government and send senators and representatives to Congress, they will be again in the position in which they were before the rebellion. Pass the constitutional amendment and that will control slavery and when the rebels cease fighting the Union will be virtually restored.

Thus the principle of the Southern theory, that " the war had been waged by the North for the avowed purpose of suppressing an insurrection of individuals, and with no idea of interfering with the rights of the states " [2] (not the

[1] *Post* and *Courier*, Sept. 4, 1863; *Am. Annual Cyclop.*, 1863, p. 625. Also *cf. supra*, ch. v.

[2] Dunning, *Essays on the Civil War and Reconstruction*, p. 102. It is interesting to compare this with the Springfield *Republican* for April 12, 1865: " We stand again on solid ground; the rebel is a citizen of the United States, to be forgiven and restored if he repents—to be excluded from all rights of citizenship if he continues obdurate. . . . The rebel state is a state of the Union, to be recovered from disloyal and placed in loyal hands."

theory of state suicide or conquered territory), was the
principle held in Massachusetts in 1865.

Yet Presidential reconstruction based on the same theory
—the existence of the states and the rebellion of citizens—
was not unquestioningly supported. The *Republican* objected because, since it believed that secession was not and
could not be a fact, it held that neither the President nor
Congress had any authority under the Constitution to propose terms of re-admission, for there was no such pre-
scribed right anywhere, strictly speaking, and " the only
legitimate reconstruction must originate with the loyal
people of the states, acting freely and of their own motion
under the state Constitutions." [1]   The Democrats immediately raised the same objection, the *Courier* arguing that
if the plan was applied in the South it might equally be
applied in the North, and if allowed, would destroy the
very germ of American liberty.[2] But by May, 1865, the
Post, in its loyalty to Johnson, expressed satisfaction in
his plan for future reorganization and belief that the government would be republican in spirit as well as in form if
the President adhered to the standard of state rights.[3]
Others continued to question the power of the President,

---

[1] April 27, 1864. In this connection a letter of Charles Francis Adams
to Richard H. Dana, Jr., is most interesting. (*Cf. supra*, ch. ii, pp. 49-
51, for position of Adams, 1860.) On April 19, 1865, Adams wrote:
" It is only as the commander of the armies of the United States that
Mr. Lincoln has the means of doing those things necessary to reëstablish order in regions where it has been violently overturned. He cannot meddle with a state as such nor prescribe any permanent form of
government for it. But he may exercise an authority which will enable the citizens of the State to reëstablish the system which has been
subverted for the moment. After this is once done his power ceases
and the machine returns to its original movements." Adams, *Dana*,
vol. ii, p. 331.

[2] *Courier*, Dec. 29, and *Post*, Dec. 12, 1863.

[3] May 29, 1865.

believing that Congress should take the initiative in such
work as this and that the President should coöperate with
the legislative branch of the government.[1] The radicals
objected to the Presidential theory because it did not appear
that universal suffrage would be accomplished by it.[2] There
were, of course, those who in their loyalty to the administration said: "Now that the proclamation of amnesty is
issued we must stand by it, no matter whether we think it
ill-advised or not."[3] They felt satisfied, however, that it
was not based upon the state-suicide theory but upon the
principle that "loyal state governments" had been subverted and that the states themselves still existed and might
resume their active functions whenever enough of the loyal
were collected to set on foot in good faith a state government.[4] Thus, except for the radical reformers, both opponents and supporters of the presidential policy consistently
adhered to one theory,—that the state could not and did
not secede, and that restoration was the work of loyal
citizens.

The radicals opposing amnesty were the champions of
Sumner's theory; anti-slavery men, jealous for the freed-
man, desired guarantees for his personal, civil and political rights. Among these were Wendell Phillips, Whittier,
Boutwell and Forbes, representative of Abolitionists and
anti-slavery Republicans, extreme and conservative. Defense of the principle of Sumner's and Stevens' theories

[1] *Commonwealth*, Dec. 11, 1863. Loring, *Reconstruction*, a pamphlet
published 1866, furnishes an able defense of Congressional reconstruction. It argues the law or the circumstances, not the necessity of the
case.

[2] Springfield *Republican*, May 18, 1864, criticizing Phillips' position.

[3] For example, the *Advertiser*, Dec. 15, 1863, and Worcester *Spy*, Oct.
19, 1863.

[4] *Advertiser*, Dec. 10, 1863.

that the slave states were merely men and territory and that rebellion had crushed all civil forms, is found only in the *Liberator*, the *Commonwealth* and the *Spy,* organs of these factions, and in speeches and letters of their leading representatives. Boutwell for example argued:

It is useless to say that the people of a State cannot destroy the State, because they have no legal right so to do. It is not a question of legal right: it is a question of fact. . . . By force of arms we have destroyed the South Carolina of the so-called Confederate States and the old state of South Carolina has not been reproduced; therefore there is no State of South Carolina as a political organization. . . . The result is. . . . South Carolina is a blank piece of paper on which may be written a new form of government.[1]

He, however, would endorse the new government made by the people of South Carolina with the consent of Congress; but the *Commonwealth* and Sumner, the *Liberator* and Wendell Phillips argued for confiscation, declaring:

In all the history of the world governments have been administered by those who owned or who had the right to own the soil. This right had been kept jealously exclusive by the lords of the South, for well they knew that if they relinquished it, their power was broken. And now just so soon as we allow the same class to recover possession of their lands, the same process will be repeated; the poor whites and, of course, the poor blacks, will be excluded from the ownership of the soil; the same oligarchy will recover the control of these states, and though we hope the rehabilitation of slavery is impossible, yet the process of pacification will be retarded years, perhaps generations.[2]

Even the non-extremist Forbes said he fully expected to

---

[1] Boutwell, *Speeches*, pp. 380-386.
[2] *Commonwealth*, Jan. 8, 1864.

see the next movement of slave holders looking to reconstruction under state rights, take such direction as would
" let them (the Southerners) establish peonage or appren-
ticeship, or something not called slavery, but really the
same old Satan. To avoid this ", he added,

we want some law confiscating all the property of those actually serving in the Rebellion, but giving the President, or
Commission, power to remit it for those who can prove they
only helped the Rebellion under coercion, also to remit it in
favor of all who owned less than 180 acres of farming land.[1]

The ultra radical was intent upon two policies: punishment by banishment and confiscation; and the constructive
scheme of colonization by loyal Northerners equipped with
seeds, ploughshares and sewing machines, and establishing
free labor, schools and town meetings.[2] The punitive note,
though at times insistent, was not continually sounded; in
fact Sumner's purpose in confiscation was to insure emancipation and break up large estates in order to secure homes
for the colored people, rather than to humiliate the South.[3]

Finally, when military campaigns were ended and reconstruction was the business in hand, it ceased to be a theoreti-
cal problem and became a practical issue. The forebod-
ings of Forbes, amply justified by subsequent events, became widespread. New " black codes " limiting the freedom of the negro, aroused apprehension lest the results, so
dearly bought, should be snatched away;[4] therefore, it was

[1] Forbes, *Letters (Supplementary)*, vol. ii, p. 339, to Captain E. B.
Ward, Dec. 29, 1864; also vol. iii, pp. 43-45, to an Editor, Aug. 6, 1865.

[2] Wendell Phillips at Cooper Institute, *Liberator*, Jan. 30, 1863; at
the Anniversary of the American Anti-Slavery Society, *Liberator*, May
19, 1865; Worcester *Spy*, April 25, 1865.

[3] *Cong. Globe*, 40 cong., 2 sess., p. 3247 (June 18, 1868) ; also Springfield *Republican*, July 1, 1865.

[4] Winthrop wrote J. P. Kennedy, July 9, 1865: " Our New England

argued, "It is our right and duty to secure whatever the public safety and the public faith require." [1] Moreover this idea soon became embodied in resolutions of the legislature, insisting, with an emphasis which the castly sacrifice of the lives of her heroes and the lavish expenditures of her means entitled Massachusetts to use, that everything should now be done to secure in peace the fruits of war.

And many who would preserve the fruits of victory came to believe in negro suffrage as a means. [2] "Give the black the ballot and he can protect himself, or if not, we shall have done the best we can to protect him," [3] was one type of argument. The theory was that freedmen made so by the fundamental law of the land would not long remain bereft of the rights of freemen. For "to suppose that the emancipated blacks of the South would not be allowed the right of suffrage was to disbelieve the honesty and deny the truth of our Republican institutions." [4] Of

people are full of apprehension that the Union is to be restored too soon, and that the Southern States are about to reorganize themselves upon their old principles." And Boutwell (*Speeches*, p. 544) said the spirit of slavery is not destroyed, and if the old local power is restored, in some form they will continue oppression of the class recently in servitude. Also, *Life of Garrison*, vol. iv, p. 94; *Liberator*, Aug. 25, 1865; *Advertiser*, May 30, 1865, Jan. 18, 1866; *Post*, May 3, 1866.

[1] Especially by Richard Henry Dana, Jr., in the Faneuil Hall meeting, June 21, 1865; Adams, *Dana*, vol. ii, p. 333. Also *Advertiser*, Jan. 18, 1866.

[2] Indeed such had become the opinion of the legislature in its resolutions of 1868: "We recognize impartial suffrage in the rebel states as an indispensable condition of permanent pacification." *Am. Annual Cyclop.*, p. 458.

[3] Forbes, *Letters* (*Supplementary*), vol. iii, p. 45, to an Editor, Aug. 6, 1865. He also said in the same letter: "I would sooner trust the most ignorant and brutal men to vote for themselves, rather than a self-styled superior class to vote for them."

[4] So argued the Hampshire *Gazette*, e. g., May 23, 1865, as had the Worcester *Spy* as early as Aug. 31, 1863.

course they confidently believed that the negro would vote
on the side of freedom and would be an ally sufficient
"to preserve our Union and our freedom from foes without
as well as foes within."

But before 1866 many of those who granted the justice
of the abstract theory felt that making immediate voters
of the freedmen was both absurd and dangerous; that they
needed the discipline of a steady rise to citizenship, a pro-
bation similar to that of the intelligent foreigners who
have emigrated thither.[1] Even loyal friends of the negro,
such as Parker Pillsbury, for a time believed voters " should
know the difference between the almanac and the Declaration of Independence." [2] The more visionary champions
of the negro, although favoring education by all practical
means, were convinced that the exercise of political rights
would most effectively accomplish this end; [3] and while
conservatives saw the danger in aligning race against race,
whites against blacks,[4] yet in time the practical difficulties
of the problem drove the party to follow its leaders and
champion the cause of the visionaries.[5] Thus the question
of what to do with the negro, which at the beginning was
separate from the question of the status of the states,[6] be-

[1] Springfield *Republican*, May 18, 1864; *Advertiser*, July 16, 1866.

[2] *Sumner MSS*, from P. Pillsbury, July 3, 1864.

[3] Sanborn, *Howe*, p. 290. Undoubtedly the view of Sanborn as well
as Howe.

[4] *E. g.*, the *Advertiser*, Aug. 8, 1865.

[5] " The collision between Johnson and Congress has settled the fate
of a good many projects, *i. e.*, the theory of making education the universal test of qualification for the suffrage, and universal civil equality.
They must be laid aside. . . . The question now is what is the best
solution to be had, not what is that which we most desire." *Advertiser*, Feb. 27, 1866.

[6] There was occasional vain hope that the negro question would settle
itself. Colonization, discussed from time to time, was given up; sep-

came, owing to circumstances, not only associated with the original question but incident to its solution; the Republican platform of Massachusetts in 1866 demanded Congressional reconstruction and impartial suffrage.

In 1865 the Republicans had stood for the Thirteenth Amendment, and expressed the universal loyalty to Johnson which supported his accession to office. They claimed to have no theories to promulgate in relation to the right of suffrage, but protested against admitting to the franchise rebel soldiers and traitorous politicians and "excluding loyal men of equal intelligence, thousands of whom have borne arms and shed their blood in the nation's defence." Their convention, however, over which Charles Sumner presided, had called upon Congress "to see to it that the loyal people, white or black, should have the most perfect guarantees for safety before any final steps were taken toward the readmission of the revolted people of the South to their forfeited rights."[1] Thus, though asserting confidence in Johnson they officially took their stand for the compromise theory, that the rights of the states were tem-

---

aration of blacks from whites was mentioned, but perceived to be impracticable. Education was advocated universally for the poor white as well as black, and looked to as a solution of the problem. The Springfield *Republican* (as early as Sept. 23, 1862) saw with almost prophetic vision "full prerogatives of citizenship, which the most ultra of their friends do not propose to bestow on them at once"; and government interference for the protection of the weaker party if the planters should not give fair wages. The rest of its vision, however, was that of the provincial New-Englander who expected with the change of the labor system a change in the structure of society: the disappearance of aristocracy and the plantation and the emergence of middle classes— traders, mechanics, cultivated men in a society like their own. Then they believed there would be unity of interest and aims, and the nation would enter upon a career of prosperity, power and glory. Similarly, Forbes to Ashburner, *Letters (Supplementary)*, vol. i, p. 326.

[1] *Advertiser*, Sept. 15, 1865; *Am. Annual Cyclop.*, 1865, p. 534.

porarily forfeited, the theory of Congressional reconstruction which evidenced jealous care for the security of victory. Addresses to the convention, however, were more bold than the platform. Alexander H. Bullock, candidate for governor, and Benjamin F. Butler, a vice-president of the convention, both urged " loyal suffrage without inequality of race or color." [1]

The justice of suffrage with an educational qualification was conceded even by the Democrats,—that was the Massachusetts standard; [2] but to insist that the people of the South should be kept out of Congress until they gave the ballot to the freedmen, was " an interference with local right and local government, revengeful and revolutionary." [3] Therefore the Democratic convention of 1865 approved of President Johnson's plan to restore the states lately in rebellion to their proper position in the Union, leaving each state to regulate the question of suffrage for itself." [4]

Moderate champions of the suffrage, in the meantime, urged that it be intelligent, if possible, but impartial at any rate. They condemned enfranchisement of the negro and disfranchisement of the Southern whites as displacing one oligarchy of race by another.[5] But extremists held that any reorganization of the rebel states which did not rest on the principles of absolute equality of every man before the law would be " a practical surrender of the North to

[1] *Advertiser,* Sept. 15, 1865, records the speeches of both.

[2] *Post,* June 5 and July 6, 1865. On July 14 it urged: " Let an amendment be adopted that the representation in Congress shall be based upon the number of legal voters, qualified by the ability to read, and the merits of negro suffrage and common schools would soon be recognized throughout the South."

[3] *Post,* Aug. 22, 1865.

[4] *Post,* Sept. 29, 1865; *Am. Annual Cyclop.,* 1865, p. 535.

[5] *E. g.,* Springfield *Republican,* Dec. 15, 1866.

the South ", and pledged themselves to agitation as devoted and tireless as that for abolition.[1]   Those, moreover, who worked diligently and effectively for enfranchisement saw it not at all as a matter of philanthropy or sentiment, but as a practical necessity for the safety of the Union and the continuance of peace, after all they had paid for it.[2]

For the education of the community on this point a suffrage meeting was held in Faneuil Hall, June 21, 1865. The Honorable Theophilus Parsons occupied the chair, John Greenleaf Whittier was a vice-president and Richard H. Dana, Jr., was chairman of a committee to prepare an address to the people of the United States urging the necessity of a reorganization of the revolted states upon just and correct principles.   John Murray Forbes, with Whittier and Charles G. Loring, were on this committee.   The meeting resolved:

That in recognizing the rebel states, the safety of loyal citizens in those states, the stability of our government and the claims of justice require that none shall be allowed to vote who are not loyal and that none shall be expelled from voting because of their race and color.

To the same end, namely, the education of the community, the Loyal Publication Society, the *Atlantic Monthly*[3] and the *North American Review*[4] argued the cause.   A *North*

---

[1] Resolution of the anti-slavery celebration at Framingham, July 4, 1865, in *Liberator*, July 20, 1865. Also in Emerson's *Journal* for Sept. 30, 1865 (1864-1876, p. 114), we find: "Sumner and his valiant young contemporaries set themselves to the task of making their views not only clear, but prevailing."

[2] Forbes, *Letters (Supplementary)*, vol. ii, p. 34, to Hugh McCulloch, July 7, 1865.

[3] *Atlantic Monthly*, Aug., 1865 and Dec., 1866.

[4] *North American Review*, April, 1865.

American article by Lowell was generous and judicious in tone and outlined in theory the policy to be pursued.

An expression of opinion even more generous and judicious than Lowell's, was embodied in Andrew's valedictory addressed to the Massachusetts legislature on January 4, 1866. He argued strongly that the main elements of Southern regeneration were to be sought in the South itself. After the anti-slavery amendment should be adopted by the legislatures he believed negro suffrage would be a question of statesmanship and not of constitutional limitation. He was sternly opposed to reorganization by the colored vote; he said: " We want the popular vote and the rebel vote is better than a loyal one, if on the right side." If the rebel vote should not be on the right side, he was not in favor of a surrender of the present rights of the Union to a struggle between a white minority aided by the freedmen on the one hand, against a majority of the white race on the other; he would not consent, having rescued these states by arms from secession and rebellion, to turn them over to anarchy and chaos.[1]

This sane, judicious estimate of the situation was merely read, complimented and forgotten;[2] John Murray Forbes confessed some years later: " Many of us, myself among the number, received this far-sighted advice with coolness or opposition; but the history of reconstruction now seems to prove conclusively, that his views were statesmanlike and

---

[1] *Senate Documents*, no. 2, Jan., 1866 (pp. 10, 11, 18).

[2] Pearson, *Life of Andrew*, vol. ii, p. 289; also Springfield *Republican*, Jan. 5, 1866: " In the whole address both in idea and spirit he has reached the *juste milieu* between the radicalism and conservatism of his own party." The *Advertiser* likewise approved; and the *Post* agreed in part: it conceded that the basis of representation to Congress should be changed from population to legal voters, but insisted that it should be done in such a way as to be in harmony with the theory that the states are still in the Union.

prophetic." [1]   To be sure, even though not heeded in 1866, Andrew's plan was more far-reaching than any generally accepted previous to this time and as such is significant. Until 1865 the universal demand had been for the restoration of those states by the loyal people thereof; [2] but Andrew would have the government of the United States require that guarantees of equal civil rights to the blacks, franchise according to laws of universal application (permitting educational qualification), annullment of secession ordinances and repudiation of rebel debt, all be put to the vote of the people themselves.   Nevertheless this comprehensive plan was ignored through shortsightedness.   A few leaders had become so obsessed with one idea, they concentrated attention on it so persistently and continually, that it blocked their mental vision; they had no perspective, no grasp of the whole situation.

Then, too, the sincere belief of these would-be preservers of the nation that it was necessary to secure the fruits of victory in order to protect the country against the recently conquered rebels, that it was necessary to secure to the negro the right and privileges of his recently acquired liberty, and that the Republican party had yet more work to do, in fact, a mission to fulfill, became in practice political capital.   It also furnished a good point of attack for the Democrats; it was easy to say that the disfranchisement of Southern whites and the enfranchisement of the blacks was advocated with the intent of keeping the party in power for the sake of the power and the advantages

[1] *Reminiscences*, vol. iii, p. 29. The Springfield *Republican*, March 18 and Sept. 11, 1867, also confessed the folly of disfranchisement of whites, and on Jan. 31, 1868, said: "No reconstruction can be permanent and successful which does not command the consent of the great body of the Southern people."

[2] *Cf. supra*, p. 149.

incident thereto.   It was so argued by the *Post*, especially
when commenting on the report of the committee of fifteen
and when attacking the Freedmen's Bureau.[1]   As to the
bureau itself, its opposition and support but illustrate the
same principles involved in every reconstruction measure.
The Democrats objected to it because it infringed " one of
the fundamental rights " of the states, that of governing
their own citizens by their own laws.[2]   The friends of the
bureau were those championing the welfare of the negro
because, in the words of Forbes, " He has no friend, no
rights that a white man is bound to respect." [3]   Even its
friends regretted its military character and certain phases
of its management; [4] but convinced of the practical necessity, they believed, as their legislature took occasion to resolve,[5] that the negro (soldiers, etc.) had a right to demand
the fullest protection from the government of the United
States.

The Republicans of Massachusetts furthermore felt their
party essential to such protection.   Indeed their convention
in 1866 made political capital of the various issues; their
resolutions recognized the fact

that all questions of reconstruction, of suffrage, of protection
to freedmen, of security to the persecuted unionists of the
South, resolve themselves into these: Shall the people who

[1] May 3, 1866, June 25, 1868.   Also *Winthrop MSS*, to J. P. Kennedy,
Aug. 12, 1866.   Indeed the *Post* (Nov. 20, 1867) said boldly: " The
single purpose is to get the State (Alabama) into negro control . . .
and upon the blacks rest the Radical plans for the perpetuity of their
present power in the nation."

[2] *Post*, Mar. 16, 1864.

[3] *Letters (Supplementary)*, vol. ii, p. 246.

[4] Andrew to Sumner, in Pearson, *op. cit.*, vol. ii, p. 274; *Advertiser*,
Dec. 16, 1865.

[5] *House Leg. Doc.*, 1866, no. 108.

saved the country still control it? Shall the soldiers of the Union, whose bravery decided on the field the fate of war . . . reap the rich results of their labors in the regenerated country? . . . Shall we reconstruct the rebels or shall they reconstruct us?[1]

PART II

POLITICAL ISSUES TO 1876

With such appeals from the Republicans, namely " Should the people who saved the country control it? ", reconstruction became definitely a question of party ascendency. The Republicans asserted that their leadership would mean confidence of the people in Congress; and they held that Congress ought to be strengthened in its work of determining under what conditions the states lately in rebellion should be restored. They approved the Fourteenth Amendment then pending before Congress and stood for the " enfranchisement of a long oppressed race and the establishment of an American and democratic policy of government ", but above all they believed it was to be the work of the Republican party. Moreover they attacked Johnson as a hindrance, accusing him of betraying the party which elected him and " of entering into a conspiracy with disloyal men, North and South, to place the country permanently in the hands of dangerous enemies of the government."[2]

In the meantime Johnson and his friends made an appeal to the country; they summoned the supporters of the President and his policy, Republicans and Democrats, to meet in a " National Union Convention " in Philadelphia. The cause of this Philadelphia convention of August 14, 1866,

[1] *Advertiser*, Sept. 14, 1866; *Am. Annual Cyclop.*, 1866, p. 478.
[2] Springfield *Republican*, Oct. 27, 1866.

made a stir in Massachusetts; a state convention to name delegates was held, ratification meetings and grand rallies followed. But by the middle of August agitation had quieted down and Warrington observed: " It looks now as if it would not result in anything very alarming. The Massachusetts delegates represent nobody."

The movement had, in fact, but faltering support from the prominent non-Democrats who were nominated vice-presidents of the state convention; and that convention of August 8 was significant for the absence of the conservative leaders, who had been expected to support this new endeavor to conciliate the factions of North and South. A contemporary report says:

The natural leaders of a conservative party in Massachusetts were conspicuously absent. Mr. Winthrop was not there, nor Mr. Ticknor, nor Judge Curtis, nor Judge Abbott, nor Mr. Ashmun, nor Caleb Cushing, nor any Lawrences, nor any Adamses, nor any Lincolns, nor a Parker, nor any of the F. F's. of Boston or the Connecticut Valley. . . . Instead there were the old hack leaders of the Democratic party—Moses Bates, Edward Avery, Richard Spofford, Chester W. Chapin, Thomas F. Plunkett, and a portion of their recruits from the old Whig and Know Nothing parties in 1862; but of Republicans who voted for Abraham Lincoln in either 1860 or 1864 hardly a dozen all told, and none of these conservative in temperament or education.[1]

The same authority discounted the claim of the convention for a full attendance; instead the report declared that only about six of the hundred western Massachusetts towns were represented and scarcely seventy-five in all.

It is thus clear that the attempt of 1866 to unite all parties was a failure. And the partisan *Advertiser* ob-

[1] *Ibid.*, Aug. 9, 1866. Similarly Warrington, *ibid.*, Aug. 18, 1866.

served sceptically, though truly, that although the new organization had managed for a second time to draw to itself some of the men who had gone into the People's party in 1862, yet the pretense of a great popular movement which calls upon all good citizens to come out from their old party lines was now " a rather stale trick "; for, it concluded, with party dogmatism, the great mass of the Republican party knew that the work of firmly establishing the Union which four years of war had secured could only be carried through by the organization under which they had acted since 1860.[1]   Here was the issue and here the explanation of the failure within Massachusetts of the cause of the Philadelphia convention.   The crux of the situation had been shrewdly pointed out even in July; the judicious *Republican* had conceded that certainly one-third of the Republican Unionists would be willing to follow Johnson against Congress.   " But to reject Thaddeus Stevens and Charles Sumner and support Mr. Johnson is one thing, and to go to bed with copperheads and rebels is another; and many eager for the first will hesitate long before doing the last." [2]

The alternative of an alliance in support of Johnson made up from all parties, an alternative evident from the membership of the convention of August 8, was an alliance between the new organization and the Democrats.   This, however, was not formally accomplished until October 4, when both conventions met in Faneuil Hall, the one at noon, the other at four o'clock.   Then the Democrats were unanimous in their support of the ticket of the " National Union Convention "; they in fact resolved that it was inexpedient in the present political crisis to make separate nominations.[3]

[1] *Ibid.*, Aug. 8, 1866.   [2] *Ibid.*, July 21, 1866.
[3] *Post*, Oct. 4, 1866.

By election day the alliance was so complete that the votes of the anti-Republicans were tabulated " Democratic ".

In the election the cause of the " National Unionists " was apparently forgotten. Although the political canvass was enlivened in the middle of September by visiting Southerners from the " Loyal Unionists " convention,[1] the campaign closed with little excitement and a light vote. Ten days before election Warrington regretted the " little activity in political affairs in this region " (Boston), and observed that in local nominations there was " very little to excite enthusiasm for or against ". On November 6 the entire Republican state ticket was reëlected by a large majority. The work and dominance of the Republican party were secured.

Meanwhile we find that the nation-stirring events that now followed and culminated in the impeachment and trial of the President were foreshadowed in the resolutions[2] of the Republican state convention of this year, 1866. In answer to the general professed loyalty of all factions to Johnson and his policies the Massachusetts Republicans had then attacked him as a hindrance to the progress of reconstruction, had accused him of betraying the party which elected him, and had claimed furthermore that he had entered into a conspiracy with disloyal men, North and South, to place the country permanently in the hands of dangerous enemies of the government.

The resolutions of 1867 went farther. They were definite in their attack; approving the measures adopted by Congress, they asserted that the short-comings of Johnson rendered his continuance in office the constant cause of the gravest anxiety, and made it imperative to employ every constitutional mode of curbing and resisting him, and, if

[1] *Advertiser*, Sept. 14, 1866.   [2] *Supra*, p. 162.

necessary, to deprive him of all power to harm. They approved therefore the measures of Congress to defeat the plans of " this dangerous and desperate man ", even to the exercise of the extraordinary power " to remove from office this destroyer of the public peace and this enemy of the Government itself." [1]

As in 1865 on the question of negro suffrage, here again speeches to the convention were more extreme than the resolutions; here again Benjamin F. Butler took the advance position, making a bold attack on the President. Henry Wilson spoke with more restraint, yet he asserted that Johnson was not carrying on the policy of Lincoln and that there was sentiment throughout the country to sustain Congress and to put down the unconstitutional assumptions of the President. Nevertheless, in spite of speeches and resolutions, and leaders such as Sumner, Wilson and Boutwell, the rank and file of the party, radical and conservative, thought impeachment useless, ungrounded and injurious. The criticism has in fact been made by contemporaries and is to be found in the press, that the people were in a shocking state of indifference as to policies; the *Republican* commented: " They are so busy earning their bread and butter and money to pay taxes, that they do not seem to care a ' red cent ' about who is governor, or president or member of Congress." [2]

The Democrats in 1867 refused to take up the issue and therefore increased the indifference concerning aggressive action against the President.[3] They said through the *Post*

[1] *Ibid.*, Sept. 12, 1867; *Am. Annual Cyclop.*, 1867, p. 482.

[2] Springfield *Republican*, Aug. 24, 1867. Similarly Worcester *Spy*, Feb. 28, 1868: "And everywhere men pursue their ordinary ways without anxiety and without distrust. . . . The Legislature continues so profoundly absorbed in deciding who shall sell rum, that it has not even heard the commotion of the elements outside."

[3] *Advertiser*, Sept. 16, 1867.

that impeachment was the business of Congress and not a popular issue in Massachusetts.[1]   In truth the general confidence in Johnson that in 1865 was a part of the loyalty of all parties to the nation in the hour of need was fast ebbing; even his advocates were coming to disapprove of his course of action [2] and were not willing to champion his cause.   The Democrats at this juncture, therefore, tried to direct attention to local issues which concerned the rights and liberties of the people of the state, declaring in the *Post*:

The people of Massachusetts were never so resolved as now to have a clear and final understanding with the ruling party on the subject of their rights, and they will not be hoodwinked or put off by any partisan buncomb aimed at the President, the dead and buried rebellion, or the Radical windmill of Justice and Liberty.[3]

The "subject of their rights" mainly concerned the liquor-license question, the issue which in 1874 was destined to bring victory to the Democrats.   But it was as yet (1867) too early to divert a campaign from national affairs.   This was made clear by the fact that the attempt to influence the Republican convention on the local issue failed.   Members of *P. L. L.*, a license organization, and the *Alliance and Templars*, a temperance organization, were present at the state convention, but they neutralized each other; and the Republican organization and national issues were left triumphant.

Yet within the Republican party impeachment was the

---

[1] Such was also the opinion of the Springfield *Republican*, Sept. 6, 1867.

[2] For example, R. C. Winthrop wrote J. P. Kennedy that the presidential tone was full of infelicities and "did away with all the good impressions which Johnson had previously made." *MSS*, Oct. 14, 1866.

[3] *Post*, Sept. 13, 1867.

propaganda of the minority. With the exception of his radical critics, in 1865 Johnson had no unyielding enemies;[1] in fact the tone of the Republican press showed a general unanimity of sentiment against impeachment throughout November and December of 1867.[2] It was really with frank reluctance that the press came later to support the movement. The *Journal* said, for example, " If it is a duty we must take it up, but that duty must be made clearer than it is now." [3] In general the policy of the newspapers was merely to record events without comment. Editorials did now and then discuss the issues: the *Republican*, for example, boasted that it had not hesitated to pronounce its disapproval of the feature of the Tenure of Office Bill which made it possible for cabinet officers, backed by Congress, to thwart the President's plans. " Such ", it said, " is not good government. It is not respectable politics. It is not even good manners." [4] Yet in the same editorial it said:

It is no matter, and nobody's business, so far as impeachment is concerned, whether it [the Tenure of Office Bill] is con-

[1] *Sumner MSS*, especially from Ben: Perley Poore (June 26, 1865), who feared that Johnson was surrounded by a set of corrupt Democratic politicians; *Garrison MSS*, Garrison to his son Wendell, April 10, 1866. The *Commonwealth* (June 17, 1865) opposed Johnson's plan because it did not include negro suffrage. Others less critical had qualms; Lawrence, for example, wrote his brother (*MSS*, April 15, 1865): " It causes alarm and humiliation to have Johnson for Prest so soon."

[2] Hampshire *Gazette*, Dec. 3, 1867; Springfield *Republican*, Nov. 30, 1867, said: " The tone of the Republican press shows unanimity against impeachment "; and the *Advertiser* agreed: " The press of the party has almost unanimously declared itself in opposition to the scheme." The Worcester *Spy*, however, with its vision colored by its earlier anti-slavery professions, urged action and regretted its failure (Feb. 25, 28, April 1, May 23, 1868).

[3] Jan. 29, 1867.

[4] Feb. 29, 1868.

stitutional or not. . . . Mr. Johnson would be just as guilty
of resisting the execution of the laws, if the bill should be
declared unconstitutional. . . . His crime lies in making himself the judge of the legality or propriety of a statute passed
over his veto. . . . No matter how clear his convictions, no
matter how honest his purpose, he is criminal if he refuses to
obey a law before the Supreme Court has passed upon it. . . .
If he can refuse to obey one law he can refuse to obey any
law.[1]

Such was the general dispassionate acquiescence and
qualified defense of the policy of Congress.   And Warrington was undoubtedly right when he shrewdly observed:

Parties, according to my observation, are governed generally
by minorities.   The abolitionists and radicals on the slavery
question have never been in a numerical majority even in the
Republican party; . . . they won their great triumphs since
1861, on the question of emancipation, negro soldiers, negro
voting and so on, by the necessity of the case, and not by con-
vincing the conservatives of the truth of their doctrines.   They
are winning the impeachment question the same way.[2]

In the end, however, the minority did not win.   The
impeachment case was lost and the conclusion of the trial
was welcomed with a sense of relief.   The resolution of
the state convention for impeachment had been obviously
the motion of its leaders and at no time was the case of
vital concern to the people of the state, and finally even
its champions recognized the advantage to the party from
its failure.[3]   There was in fact a universal satisfaction

---

[1] With more vehemence on the same point, Hampshire *Gazette*, Feb.
25, 1868.

[2] Springfield *Republican*, Sept. 14, 1867.

[3] J. M. Forbes (*Letters and Recollections*, vol. ii, p. 165) to W. P.
Fessenden, May 23, 1868, said he did not believe it was worth the

among Republicans that Congress could thenceforth attend to its legislative business and that in November the country could render its verdict on the President.[1]   The Democrats, who had condemned the radicals leading the impeachment, were also satisfied with acquittal; they too looked to the coming election, not for a judgment on Johnson but for the demolition of the radical party.

The anticipated election of the presidential year 1868 dealt but incidentally with Johnson; it was in the main a contest for party permanence.   The speeches of Rice and Boutwell at the Republican convention waived all questions of detail, state and national, and stood upon the platform of "loyalty to the republic and fidelity to the rights of man"; in other words, they stood for the Republican party, which they believed patriotic and consistent, and against the Democratic party, which they believed inconsistent, impatient, and wrong.   The delegates at the convention approved the Chicago platform; they approved Congressional reconstruction as wise and good; they praised Sumner's "eloquent, fearless and persistent devotion to the sacred cause of human rights", and called for his reelection.[2]   The state acquiesced by a rousing vote in favor of Grant, every county and every district giving majorities comparable to those of 1860 and 1864; with his military prestige, Grant kept the Republicans in power in both state and nation.

Reverberation of the party antagonism of 1868 was still

breaking-up of the Republican party, "the only bulwark of freedom," because, he argued, "We owe it to the living and to the dead to keep together until we have absolutely secured the fruits of our dearly-bought victories." Similarly *Sumner MSS*, from Henry I. Bowditch, May 18, 1868; Springfield *Republican* and *Advertiser*, May 18, 1868.

[1] Springfield *Republican*, May 27, 1868.

[2] *Ibid.*, Sept. 10, 1868; *Am. Annual Cyclop.*, 1868, p. 460.

evident in the campaign of the next year. The Republican
convention in fact resolved that the Democratic party, " by
its close alliance with the slave power during the whole
generation, its sympathy with the public enemies during the
late Civil War, its constant endeavors to perpetuate disorder in the rebel states ", had " forfeited forever all
claims to the confidence of the people, and could not without great peril to their liberties and fortunes be entrusted
with the government of the nation or of this commonwealth." [1]   But in 1870 a change was apparent. The state
convention did not attack its opponent; instead, it devoted
itself to its own affairs, congratulated the Republicans of
the country on the adoption of the Thirteenth, Fourteenth
and Fifteenth Amendments, and approved " the vigorous
and successful administration of General Grant "; it then
turned its attention to local issues that had been arising and
increasing in number and strength since 1865, or since the
entire energy of the people had become no longer necessary
for the preservation of the Union.

The Democrats in the meantime, beginning in 1865, had
argued persistently for state rights. Like a refrain they
repeated their theory: " Each state in the Union is free,
sovereign and independent and entitled to exercise and enjoy every power, jurisdiction and right which is not ex-
pressly delegated to the General Government in the Constitution of the United States." [2]   In 1868 they added a
definite though futile attack on the party in power because,
they said:

The leaders of the Republican party in Congress had shown a
consistent and persistent purpose to usurp all the powers and

---

[1] *Advertiser*, Sept. 23, 1869; *Am. Annual Cyclop.*, 1869, p. 416.

[2] *Post*, Oct. 2, 1867. From resolutions of the Democratic State Convention.

functions of all the other departments of the Government; to trample on the constitution in order to organize a squad of negro colonies dependent on themselves, by whose aid to perpetuate their own political power.[1]

But the following year (1869), although they asserted that they still adhered to the principles of Democracy, they deemed it a political duty to acquiesce in settled results and postpone fruitless opposition to the accomplished facts of yesterday in order to secure effective action upon the pressing problems of the day.[2]   And in 1871[3] the Springfield convention accepted the amendments, pledging itself " to maintain in good faith the Constitution in all its parts and in all its provisions."   It acquiesced in things as they were, it accepted the work of the party in power; but all the while it remained true to its refrain, its fundamental principle, and consistently protested against " the persistent invasion of local self-government by Congress," and asked that the Constitution be " strictly construed in the interest of the rights reserved to the States as well as those delegated to the general Government." [4]

The nation-wide attack on the administration which came in 1872, although it had the support of the Democratic organization of Massachusetts, was not of a piece with previous attacks of the party upon the Republicans.   The Liberal Republican movement in theory had a great many champions who condemned the extreme policy and the cor-

[1] *Post*, Sept. 3, 1868; *Am. Annual Cyclop.*, 1868, p. 459.

[2] *Post*, Aug. 25, 1869; *Am. Annual Cyclop.*, 1869, p. 415.

[3] Criticism and opposition to definite policies were heard in 1870; but the resolution "that the thirteenth, fourteenth and fifteenth amendments to the Constitution of the United States are unconstitutionally proposed and null and void," was referred to committee and not embodied in the platform (*Post*, Oct. 13, 1870).

[4] *Post*, Sept. 14, 1891; *Am. Annual Cyclop.*, 1871, p. 493.

ruptions of the party they had helped to maintain in power for a dozen years. There were also men of the anti-slavery group who on all other questions were democratic in their theories and who now felt that it was time to turn to other issues, such as free trade and civil service reform, and away from the party that had served their ideal but had become corrupt. There was still a third group who changed allegiance for personal reasons; these were largely the friends of Sumner, who resented the treatment he had received at the hands of the executive and the consequent loss to prestige of the Massachusetts senator. To these later on were added the Democrats; but for the present attention may be confined to the Republicans.

For each group we might name typical representatives. For the idealists in pure politics and less centralized administration, Charles Francis Adams, Warrington, and among newspapers, the Springfield *Republican* may be chosen; for the anti-slavery group, some of whom were Democratic idealists, William Schouler, Warrington, and Francis W. Bird; and for the anti-Grant pro-Sumner company, Francis W. Bird, leader of a goodly company of less conspicuous anti-slavery men and Abolitionists. But when we have named the conspicuous we find the reasons for their allegiance overlapping, and when we follow them from theory into the realities of the campaign we find their allegiance shifting.

The theory of a Liberal Republican movement was one thing, the nomination of Greeley was another. Warrington, for example, was ridiculed as one who would have died for the Cincinnati cause, but whose personal hostility to Greeley denied him " the sweet boon of martyrdom ".[1] But his opposition was broader than personal feeling. Both

---

[1] Springfield *Republican*, July 26, 1872.

Warrington and Charles Francis Adams, Jr., saw and spoke of the incongruity of either Democrats or Republicans supporting Greeley. Adams explained clearly and at length his own reasons for turning from the reform movement, and, judging from the comments of numerous more humble contemporaries, his was probably the opinion of many others. " We went to Cincinnati ", said Adams,

in open revolt against the party manipulations of Messrs. Conklin and Cameron and Morton and Chandler; when we got there we were met by Messrs. Fenton, Cochrane, . . . and they with Frank Blair, kindly proceeded to " manage " things for us in the good old way. . . . I prefer the old set. . . . We went protesting against " carpet-bagism ", and they " carpet-bagged " our convention. . . . We went calling for free trade, and they gave us the most notorious and consistent protectionist in all America. We went crying out against centralization, and saying, " the world is governed too much ", and we came back with the great apostle of unlimited legislation on all conceivable subjects for our chosen candidate.[1]

Francis W. Bird and others burning for vengeance for their beloved senator were willing to ignore the incongruities that baffled such as Adams and enter the campaign on the personal issue alone. The Springfield *Republican* and individuals who were like minded, also remained loyal to the new movement, not, however, to avenge Sumner, but in protest against a party too long in power and against a political machine. Thus there were really two motives holding Republicans to the new movement,—purity in politics and vengeance for Sumner. Perhaps the whole movement may have resolved itself into anti-Grantism.

[1] Speech of Adams, Jr., quoted in the Springfield *Republican*, Oct. 1, 1872.

Allegiance to the Republican party had also, to a degree, a personal basis, but here the basis was both support of Grant and opposition to Greeley. Even so pronounced an anti-Republican as Robert C. Winthrop did not believe there was any safety in Greeley, and finally aligned himself with George B. Loring, who had shifted to the Republican party more than four years before. The conspicuous and undoubtedly the humble found themselves in queer company. As champions of Grant and Wilson, for example, there were Benjamin F. Butler, Breckinridge Democrat in 1860, Robert C. Winthrop, Constitutional Unionist in 1860 and Democrat in 1864, George B. Loring, who had been with Butler in 1860 but a Republican elector 1868, and John Murray Forbes, consistently, persistently though not uncritically Republican throughout. And, on the other hand, Bird, Sumner, Schouler,—Abolitionist, anti-slavery Republican and regular Republican,—found themselves organized with the war Democrats and the pro-slavery Democrats.

We have been considering representative individuals; as to political organization, the reform movement of 1872 had the fate of the People's party of 1862 and the " National Unionist " movement in 1866: in the end it became merged with the Democratic party. The Liberal Republican and the Democratic state conventions met on the same day, committees from both conventions conferred and reported nominations which were accepted with enthusiasm by both conventions; Charles Sumner was named for governor.[1] Then followed a joint session addressed by ex-governor Banks, who hoped that the day would soon come when every vestige of military power and military authority would disappear from the government. The combined conventions adopted resolutions approving the Cincinnati and Balti-

---

[1] *Post*, Sept. 12, 1872.

more platform, attacking Grant's administration, endorsing
Greeley and Brown, praising Sumner, with an enumeration
of his achievements.

Thus far Francis W. Bird was successful. It is claimed
by Boutwell in his *Reminiscences*, that Bird had much to
do with Sumner's decision to join the Liberal movement.[1]
Whether that is true or not, it is clear, as Bird pointed out,
that Sumner adhered to the new party when two things
were determined upon, " the protection of the colored race,
and the defeat of Grant." [2]   And soon after Sumner had
advised the colored citizens of Boston to vote for Greeley,
(thus making public his position), Bird and others of the
State central committee of the new party issued an address
to " those Liberal Republicans of Massachusetts who felt
it their duty to separate from the regular Republican organization ".   The address referred to the warfare made
upon the Massachusetts senator and condemned the President and his advisers.   It declared that Grant had been a
pro-slavery Democrat and that Greeley was an anti-slavery
man and a founder of the Republican party.[3]   When the
Liberal Republican convention met Bird was temporary
chairman; he suggested the conference committee, and was
on that committee; his hero, Sumner, was nominated for
governor, and Sumner's achievements were enumerated in
the resolutions.   Bird, in turn, was nominated elector at
large, and on the refusal of Sumner to be the candidate for
governor, was named in his place.   Thus through the pre-
liminaries of the campaign, through party organization and

---

[1] *Reminiscences*, vol. i, p. 230.

[2] *Post*, Sept. 12, 1872; speech of Bird in Ward 11, Boston.

[3] *Ibid.*, Aug. 6, 1872. It is interesting to note that in May, Bird had
boasted his sympathy with Democratic ideas on all topics but slavery
and railroad incorporation. Springfield *Republican*, May 27, 1872.

nominations, the chairman of the Liberal Republican state committee had been a successful director. But he could not lead the voters generally.

The Liberal cause in Massachusetts was never full of vitality; the campaign was in fact less exciting here than in many other states. Many Republicans throughout the state were disappointed in Grant and saw the mistakes of his administration, and had Adams been nominated at Cincinnati he might have swung the state to the reform movement; but the majority were not ready to trust Greeley. Dissatisfaction with Grant and distrust of Greeley, therefore, took all enthusiasm from the campaign. The Springfield *Republican*, however, talked loud and long and zealously for the Liberal party. To be sure, that judicious sheet early disclaimed being a Greeley organ, and conceded that there was really no quarrel over the efficiency of Governor Washburn.[1] Nevertheless in spite of these qualifications it championed the new movement so persistently that there is a vague general impression that western Massachusetts went for Greeley in 1872.

This is far from the facts. Statistics show that in the eleventh district, which included Springfield, only three towns, all in Berkshire county, went for Greeley, and these by small majorities; Otis, 66 to 65, Alford 43 to 30 and Hinsdale 139 to 129. All the Hampden county towns of the district went for Grant; and the total vote stood 11,962 for Grant to 6,918 for Greeley.[2] The tenth district included fifty-one towns of Hampshire, Franklin and Worcester counties, all largely within the influence of the *Republican*. Of these only one, Blackstone of Worcester county (on the Rhode Island border), gave a majority for

[1] Springfield *Republican*, June 12 and Aug. 29, 1872.
[2] *Post*, Nov. 6, and Springfield *Republican*, Nov. 7, 1872.

Greeley.   The total vote of the district was 14,958 for Grant and 4,398 for Greeley.   Of the whole state Greeley carried not a single district or county; but the Liberals elected one state senator and twenty-four representatives out of 235.   The Republican itself editorially acknowledged, " It is not often that any party sweeps the western counties so clearly in senators and representatives as the Republicans have done now.   It is a repetition of 1860 and 1864." [1]   The total vote of the state was about 6000 less than in 1868, Grant's vote was about 7000 less than in that year, and the Liberal and Democratic vote was almost the same as the Democratic of that year.   Grant's majority in 1872 was 72000 or (in round numbers) 69 per cent of the total vote, as compared with the Republican majority of 70 per cent in 1868, 72 per cent in 1864 and 70 per cent in 1860.[2]

The Republican party seemed firmly grounded in Massachusetts and yet in two years the state was to have a Democratic governor.   The shifting of party allegiance which was so remarkable in such men as Winthrop, Bird, Sumner and Schouler, was only symptomatic for the future; it broke the hard and fast party lines.   This shifting was indeed the beginning of deflection of Republicans, especially the ante-bellum anti-slavery men, to the Democratic party.   It was brought about largely because they believed in free-trade and civil-service reform and were also the friends of local self-government, and opposed the corruptions of the party in power.   The negro was legally and theoretically secured in his rights and privileges, and therefore Democratic theories in other lines asserted themselves.   Local issues, moreover, came to the front; and it was in them

[1] Springfield *Republican*, Nov. 6, 1872.

[2] *Cf.* Chart, appendix i.

that the voters, having had experience in shifted allegiance in 1872, shifted again and voted the Democratic ticket. That episode will be treated in its chronological sequence. For the present, before leaving entirely all reconstruction issues, it may be well to note what had been accomplished by the majority in Congress and the state.

The Thirteenth Amendment became law on December 18, 1865. In Massachusetts it had been ratified on February 2, 1865,[1] " by a unanimous yea and nay vote in both branches of the legislature ",[2] and its final adoption was approved by all the newspapers. The *Post* went so far as to say that it

should gratify everyone who desires to see the end of a social institution which has been a bar to the progress of the white population among whom it existed, a limitation to the hopes of the blacks, and a source of political trouble for a long course of years. Its ratification we have long advocated.[3]

Acquiescence in the policy of the amendment was so general that the announcement of its final adoption made little stir.[4]

Sentiment regarding the Fourteenth Amendment was not so unanimous. In the senate the following resolution was reported:

Whereas, the constitutional amendment now proposed by Congress is unsound and dangerous in principle, since, practically speaking, it allows the white race of the rebel territory of the United States, by itself and alone, to constitute and organize states, and concedes to such states the right to disfranchise

[1] *Acts and Resolves*, 1865, ch. xi, p. 445.
[2] Andrew's telegram to the President.
[3] Dec. 20 and Sept. 21, 1865.
[4] *Advertiser*, Dec. 20, 1865.

races and classes of men for capricious reasons, . . . Resolved, that to ratify said amendment, is consenting to the re-establishment of that very aristocracy—a white man's government —out of which grew the rebellion.[1]

A committee in the house made a similar report.[2]   But though the jealous fear of the extremists for the welfare of the negro thus manifested itself, the majority were not so minded; the amendment was ratified on March 20, 1867.[3]

Outside the legislature the opposition of the Democrats to this amendment, as to the Civil Rights Bill in 1866, was on their fundamental principle of state authority.   It was from this point of view that the *Post* said:

When this amendment shall become law, so thoroughly will self-government have passed away from the people of this state, that future eulogists of monarchy will refer to this vote of Massachusetts acknowledging the incapacity of her people, juries and courts to enforce equality and justice among her citizens, as pointing the moral of the incapacity of man for self-government.[4]

On the whole, however, there was surprisingly little general

[1] *Senate Legislative Documents*, 1867.

[2] *House Legislative Documents*, 1867, no. 149, Feb. 28, 1867. The majority of four were Francis W. Bird, Edwin L. Barney, Oliver H. P. Browne, Edwin G. Walker—all of earlier abolitionist sympathies. The minority of three was led by George B. Loring, now in the Republican ranks. *Cf.* Worcester *Spy,* Mar. 2, 1867; its own dissatisfaction was expressed June 16, 1866.

[3] *Acts and Resolves*, 1867, pp. 787, 788.

[4] Jan. 17, 1867. On Mar. 29, 1866, in reference to Civil Rights Bill, the *Post* remarked: " Such a measure is a bold attempt under the pretext of securing their rights to a class just emerging from a state of slavery to a state of freedom, to set aside State authority altogether, to make state officials from Governors down to those engaged in the commonest avocations abject instruments of a controlling party in Congress."

discussion. It was the affair of the legislature,—it did not touch the people of Massachusetts directly; they had elected their representatives and to them the problems of government were left.

In time the Fifteenth Amendment was presented. It apparently satisfied the most of those who had doubted the efficiency of the Fourteenth,[1] and it was adopted by the senate on March 9 and by the house on March 12, 1869. The vote in the former was 36 to 2, in the latter 192 to 15 (33 not voting).[2] Comments were few, as on the Fourteenth Amendment. The *Post* declared that it was a party measure to serve party ends, and could not see why there could not be an educational qualification.[3] But there was no aggressive protest. Neither was there much enthusiasm. To be sure the *Commonwealth* exulted: " 'Tis done, the great transaction's done!" But the *Advertiser*, representative of the Republican majority, expressed merely complacent satisfaction that the amendment would put an end to all the woes and leave the national energies free to adjust the disturbed industries of the country, and to unite in ministering to its highest prosperity and happiness.[4] Acquiescence in the work of Congress was evidently a reality, which found open acknowledgment on the part of the Democrats in their platforms of 1869 and 1871.

In the meantime new issues had stirred the state, issues that concerned the people directly. By 1870, in fact, three

[1] A few finding voice in the *Commonwealth* regretted that the amendment did not recognize the right of the colored man to hold office, but hoped for the best from its operation (Mar. 6, 1869).

[2] *Acts and Resolves*, 1869, p. 825. McPherson, *Political History of Reconstruction*, p. 493. The legislature elected in 1868 was composed of 38 Republican and 2 Democratic senators; 224 Republican and 16 Democratic representatives.

[3] *Post*, Mar. 2, 1869, and April 11, 1870.

[4] Jan. 25 and March 1, 1869, and April 1, 1870.

new parties were organized, those of Prohibition, Labor Reform and Woman Suffrage.

Agitation on the temperance question was indeed heard as soon as the war was ended. For eleven years Massachusetts had had a prohibitory law,[1] but by 1866 violations of it and resistance to it began to attract attention, for in that year nearly half of all the prosecutions in the state were for maintaining liquor nuisances. Moreover a test case came before the Supreme Court of the United States: John McGuire, convicted of selling liquor contrary to the state law, claimed that he was licensed to sell liquors as a wholesale dealer under the congressional act providing for internal revenue. The Supreme Court sustained the ruling of the state court that the federal license did not give the accused the right to sell liquor in violation of the state statutes.[2] Thereafter numerous petitions came to the legislature protesting against the law, and a committee was consequently appointed to investigate. In time it reported that the law was an infringement of personal rights; it also submitted evidence to show that intemperance had increased and that the contraband trade was in an inferior quality of liquor which added to the injurious effect of drinking, and it concluded with the recommendation for a license system. The legislature, however, rejected the recommendation and retained the old law.

But the continuous difficulty of enforcing the law agitated the people to such an extent that the question was considered by the state conventions the next year, 1867. The Republican resolution disclaiming all responsibility for the

[1] This law prohibited the sale of liquor as a beverage, and forbade the sale for mechanical or medicinal purposes except by agents of the state appointed for that purpose.

[2] *Am. Annual Cyclop.*, 1866, p. 476. A decision in keeping with the theory of Massachusetts on the general policy of Reconstruction.

enactment and retention of the prohibitory law was lost in committee; and the Democrats applied their traditional principle of "opposition to all legislation that infringes upon the private rights and liberties of the citizens ".[1]   In the meantime the advocates of prohibition organized in a State Temperance convention, which appealed to the people of Massachusetts to urge their senators and representatives to be true to the cause of prohibition.   At the election the liquor question could not be ignored.   But it was made an individual, not a party, test.   The elected legislators were pledged, irrespective of party, as follows: in the senate thirty-one for and nine against license, in the house one hundred eighty-four for and fifty against, six being uncertain.[2]

A license system was of course enacted.[3]   But the state was no better satisfied: Governor Claflin in fact reported that the prisons, jails and reformatories were filled as a result of the new law.   Another State Temperance convention met in protest.   The Democrats discussed the situation: they denied any responsibility for the law, but were still persuaded of the wisdom of some regulation of the sale of liquors other than prohibition.   The Republican resolutions again ignored the issue.[4]

But the experiment of 1868 and the consequent dissatisfaction ended in a reënactment of the prohibitory law.[5] Nevertheless dissatisfaction continued, with the result that

---

[1] In 1866 also the Democratic platform had protested against the prohibitory liquor law. *Post*, Oct. 4.

[2] *Am. Annual Cyclop.*, 1867, pp. 481 and 483.

[3] *Acts and Resolves*, 1868, ch. cxli, pp. 107-115.

[4] *Am. Annual Cyclop.*, 1868, pp. 457 and 460; *Post*, Sept. 3, 1868; *Advertiser*, Sept. 9, 1868.

[5] *Acts and Resolves*, 1869, ch. ccccxv, p. 706 *et seq.*

the majority of the new members elected to the legislature
(of 1870) were supposed to favor the sale of liquor under
proper restricton.   They amended the law so as to permit
the sale of ale, porter, cider, strong beer and lager beer, in
towns and cities that did not prohibit such sale.[1]   In the
succeeding year (1871) the question occupied less attention:
legislative action reversed the law by forbidding the sale
of intoxicating liquor unless permitted by the vote of
people in the different towns and cities.[2]

The organized protests of the Prohibitionists proved
vain.   In convention they therefore resolved, "That the
organization of an independent political party making the
suppression of the liquor traffic an avowed issue is an indispensable necessity."   Their first nominee for governor
(1870) was Wendell Phillips.[3]

The Labor Reform party had been organized the previous
year.   Agitation for the regulation of the hours of labor
and incorporation of trade unions had been heard for some
time.   As early as 1865 the Democratic platform claimed
to sympathize with any measure by which the true interests
of employer and employed could be promoted and secured;[4]
and in 1868 the same party more definitely resolved that
"the rights of labor be fully maintained, and every possible opportunity of individual improvement secured by
just laws to the workingmen of the country."[5]   But resolutions of a party not in power were entirely ineffective.
The legislature in 1866 had definitely refused any interfer-

---

[1] *Acts and Resolves*, 1870, ch. ccclxxxix, p. 298; *Am. Annual Cyclop.*,
1870, p. 470.

[2] *Acts and Resolves*, 1871, ch. cccxxxiv, p. 667; *Am. Annual Cyclop.*,
1871, p. 491.

[3] *Post*, Aug. 18, 1870; *Am. Annual Cyclop.*, 1870, p. 473.

[4] *Post*, Sept. 29, 1865.

[5] *Ibid.*, Sept. 3, 1868.

ence with the hours of labor,[1] and the organization of the
Knights of St. Crispin, the largest trade union in the state,
was refused a charter until 1870, when it was recognized
merely as a charitable institution with a right to invest its
funds in coöperative associations.[2]   Finally, therefore, in
1869, a definite party was organized to accomplish labor reform in Massachusetts.   A meeting of the friends of labor
was called on May 27; they met again in non-political
convention August 25 and 26, passing resolutions of sympathy with a recent Philadelphia meeting and the forming
of state labor associations for the better advancement of
their cause.[3]   At length on September 28, they met in political convention, nominating E. M. Chamberlin as candidate for governor.   On a platform reaffirming the principles of the Declaration of Independence, that " all men
are created free and equal ", they asked for associations of
working men or women, founded for promoting their moral
and national interests, the " same chartered rights and
privileges at the hands of legislators, State and National,
as are granted associations of capital ".   They demanded
a ten-hour day in factories and workshops.   They also
endorsed the demand of the National Labor Congress, for
the creation of a Department of Labor at Washington to
aid in protecting the rights and interests of labor.[4]

Again in 1870 and in 1871 the Labor Reformers met in
special convention and nominated state officers.[5]   They re-

---

[1] *Am. Annual Cyclop.*, 1866, p. 474.

[2] *Ibid.*, 1870, p. 470. The Knights of St. Crispin were a boot-and-shoe
union that obtained great influence for the passage of the ten-hour law
of 1874.

[3] *Post*, Aug. 26 and 27, 1869.

[4] *Advertiser*, Sept. 29, 1869; *Am. Annual Cyclop.*, 1869, p. 416.

[5] In 1870 the Labor Reformers joined the Prohibitionists in naming
Wendell Phillips for governor; in 1871 they returned to their former
candidate.

peated their resolutions of 1869, but added a plank on national finances. They would have the debt speedily paid and held that legal tender government notes were the best and safest currency.[1] This is the only party resolution passed in Massachusetts against specie payment. The question was really not an issue for that state. In fact the newspapers, from West to East,—*Republican, Spy, Post, Advertiser* and *Commonwealth;* Sumner's varied correspondents, especially J. M. Forbes, Amos A. Lawrence, C. E. Norton, and F. W. Bird; and the Democratic nominee for governor (1868) J. Q. Adams,—all declared for sound money. Benjamin F. Butler probably persuaded some to his way of thinking but, although the *Advertiser*[2] confessed that it was not disposed to deny the ability or audacity of General Butler, there is no evidence that his theories had any wide acceptance.

The Labor movement *per se*, however, was strong enough to get recognition in the resolutions of the leading parties, in both 1869 and 1870. Moreover it elected state senators and representatives: in 1869 one senator and twenty-two representatives, in 1870 eleven representatives. And the votes for its gubernatorial candidate, though not pretentious, did have an effect on the Republican majority. In 1869 there were only 13,561 Labor votes as against 74,106 Republican and 50,701 Democrats; in 1870 the joint vote of Labor and Prohibition totaled but 21,946 as compared to 79,549 Republicans and 48,536 Democrats; in 1871 again the 6848 Labor and 6598 Prohibition totaled only 13,346 to 75,129 Republican and 47,799 Democrat. Yet reducing these figures to approximate percentages, we have for the three years, 1869-1871, this result:

[1] *Am. Annual Cyclop.*, 1870, p. 474.

[2] Jan. 13, 1869.

10% (Labor)	36% (Democrat)	54% (Republican)
16%	31%	53%
10%	35%	55%.

This shows that Labor and Prohibition helped to lessen appreciably the Republican majority which in the presidential years 1868 and 1872 was 69 per cent.[1] Viewing them therefore from the standpoint of the presidential election of 1872 they appear to be but eddies in the political current, for in that year no nominations were made.[2] But viewed from future events, the temporary strength of anti-Republicans and non-Republicans was the beginning of the permanent lessening of Republican prestige.

The third new issue that concerned the people directly, namely, the question of woman suffrage, was definitely brought before the state by the presentation of a petition to the legislature in 1868. A motion to refer it to the judiciary committee with instructions to report a bill granting the right requested, failed by a vote of 119 to 74.[3] The reformers then organized, and state conventions were held in 1870 and 1871. They nominated no candidates, but passed resolutions and drew up memorials which were presented to the leading parties. These were not ignored. Although the Republican platform of 1870 was silent on the subject, there was a strong movement for it in the convention: the resolution favoring enfranchisement of women being lost only by 139 to 196. Its opponents argued successfully that the question had not been discussed by the constituencies and therefore the delegates could not know the will of the people, and also that it would be unwise to distract attention from the big issues.[4] The Labor Reformers (1871), however, by vote of 120 to 85, recognized

[1] *Cf.* graph, appendix i.   [2] *Post*, Aug. 22, 1872.

[3] *Am. Annual Cyclop.*, 1868, p. 459.

[4] *Advertiser*, Oct. 6, 1870, gives account of the motions made.

woman's right to the ballot and demanded equal pay for equal work.[1] The Democrats on the other hand said it was necessary to remove property qualifications and other limitations before considering woman suffrage, and in 1871 John Q. Adams, their nominee for governor, came out openly against it.[2] But the resolutions and memorials of the suffragists were, in fact, so well received that in the legislature of 1870 the Republican majority of the senate recognized the fitness of women to hold offices of political importance,[3] and in the house it defeated the suffrage amendment only by the vote of the speaker.

These eddies in the political current the Republican party persistently tried to avoid. In 1866 it enunciated its program. The state convention, in answer to the growing demands of labor and prohibition, resolved that questions of state and municipal administration must still in large degree be held subordinate to those greater questions of national policy which agitate and interest the people of the whole country alike.[4] In keeping with this theory the resolutions on local issues were sent to committees or ignored for some time. But one after another forced recognition (though in very vague terms) : labor reform in 1868, the temperance issue in 1870, and woman suffrage finally in 1871, when the Republican convention characteristically conceded that " the subject of suffrage for woman

[1] *Am. Annual Cyclop.*, 1871, p. 494; *Post*, Oct. 5, 1871; also *Am. Annual Cyclop.*, 1872, p. 503.

[2] *Post*, Oct. 30, 1871.

[3] Statement hereof in suffrage memorial and Republican resolutions, 1870. (*Advertiser*, Oct. 6, 1870, and *Am. Annual Cyclop.*, 1870, p. 493.) The courts, however, later ruled that Mrs. Julia Ward Howe and Mrs. Stevens had no legal authority to exercise any of the functions of justice of the peace, to which office they had been appointed by Governor Claflin. *Am. Annual Cyclop.*, 1871, pp. 491 and 492.

[4] *Advertiser*, Sept. 14, 1866.

is a question that deserves the most careful and respectful consideration ".[1] In 1871, however, and again in 1873 Benjamin F. Butler, within the party, championed all the new causes it had tried to ignore. He hoped thus to center interest in himself, their champion. Consequently the party that had avoided the eddies here and there, and had pursued its course serenely was flung into a veritable whirlpool. Yet by shrewd management it was steered safely through on its accustomed course, " the greater questions of national policy."

The Butler episodes, that of 1871 in particular, are dramatic, humorous, lamentable,—dramatic, in that one man could defy the political organization and unaided by the press gain a following which threatened to control the party; humorous, in view of our present knowledge, in that Benjamin F. Butler should have stood for prohibition and reform, attacking the extravagance and corruption of the the state administration; lamentable, in that on equivocal statements a man could gain so great a following and arouse an opposition which in its antagonism to him defended things as they were and consequently prevented any movement toward reform that perchance might have developed.

Preliminary to the campaign of 1871, when it was rumored that Governor Claflin was not putting himself forward for renomination, Benjamin F. Butler wrote a letter declaring his intention to run for the nomination. It was an answer to questions addressed to him by the Springfield *Sunday Chronicle.*[2] The questions, it is claimed, were suggested that the letter might be written in which Butler might declare his intentions. The main point of the letter con-

---

[1] *Ibid.*, Sept. 28, 1871; *Am. Annual Cyclop.*, 1871, p. 493.

[2] Both the questions and the letter were quoted in the papers throughout the state, in the Springfield *Republican* on July 17, 1871.

cerned the prohibition law. He held that if a law was on the statute books it should be enforced and therefore he would enforce it. This declaration was universally, scornfully criticized; in fact, at the end of a week after the publication of the letter the Springfield *Republican* noted that everybody, excepting a few disorganizers and federal office holders, was " merry over the complete failure of the big Butler movement thus far ", and that except in Essex county, Butler's home, the manifesto was very coldly received.[1]

But the general was undaunted. In the month intervening before the state convention he made twenty-two speeches, in which he attacked the extravagance of the state administration [2] and called for reform in the legislature, laws and party.[3] He added one issue after another until he had a wide platform including all possible planks, both new and popular: he appeared to favor labor reform, woman suffrage, prohibition; he even suggested that the idea of tariff to protect the laboring man was illusory; [4] and he finally defended specie payment.[5] In the main, however, he championed local issues, and his position was stated with Delphic skill. In the manufacturing center of Lawrence, for example, he voiced their questioning: he asked what argument there could be on the part of Republicans for opposing labor-reform measures. And he answered, " Humanity, judgment, reason, candor and the well-being of the states—all are in favor of some legislation for the laboring man." [6]

[1] July 24, 1871.

[2] *Post,* Sept. 14, 1871, at Hyde Park; *Ibid.,* Aug. 24, and *Advertiser,* Aug. 25, 1871, at Springfield.

[3] *Post,* Sept. 15, 1871, at Athol and North Adams.

[4] *Ibid.,* Aug. 24, 1871, at Springfield.

[5] *Ibid.,* Sept. 1, 1871, at Clinton.

[6] *Post,* Sept. 17, 1871.

In the western part of the state he made other generaliza-
tions on the subject. Labor reform, he told his Springfield audience, was only advanced Republicanism: now that
they had settled the question of slave labor, " why should
not the Republican party still go forward and adjust, settle
and define the exact relations of labor and capital and protect the ill-paid and overworked laborer?" [1] On the subject of woman-suffrage he was equally indefinite. He told
a Worcester audience that women had the right to the suffrage " whenever they choose to demand it." [2]

Such statements as these inevitably provoked discussion.
His promise that prohibition should be enforced everywhere if the people wanted it,[3] drew from Warrington,
for example, a letter to the Boston *Journal* exposing the
fallacy of supposing that this assertion was made, as appeared on the surface, in the interest of temperance. He
said the pledge to enforce the prohibitory law was really a
license measure, for when the law was really enforced the
people would not stand it and there would be a reversion
to license.[4] Butler's criticisms of the administration were
also refuted, not, however, because of their equivocations,
but because of their misstatements of fact. The *Advertiser,*
for example, pointed out two or three of the most striking
instances:

The commissioners on street railways, during the short time
they were in office, are charged with receiving twenty or
twenty-five dollars a day. The fact that they never received
a farthing from the State treasury, but were paid by assess-
ment on the railway companies, is suppressed. The expenses

[1] *Post*, Aug. 24, 1871.
[2] *Ibid.*, Aug. 31, 1871.
[3] *Ibid.*
[4] Quoted by the Springfield *Republican*, July 25, 1871.

of the board of education are given at $18,311.98, but no mention is made of the fact that it is mainly paid from the income of a trust fund established for the purpose, and not from the treasury. The expenses of the insurance commissioners are given at $20,119.38; but the fact is suppressed that the income of the department for the same time was $34,902.96, the surplus accruing to the treasury amounting to nearly $15,000.[1]

The campaign thus became heated. And although the press would not support Butler and, with the exception of the *Post*, did not give many of his speeches in full, yet they gave him publicity by their refutations. The *Post*, moreover, commented on the campaign: " The crack of the whip is loud and startling "; and later explained figuratively: " In the mouth of Benjamin's sack the President has placed the silver cup of official favor, and who so bold, so reckless of party discipline, as to refuse to receive him whose broad back bears all their party hopes and promises." [2] Such statements were in turn denied by the regular Republicans.

But the censure of the Republican press and its refutations were not completely effective. An animated canvass was succeeded by the following results: a majority of the ward meetings in Boston footed up in Butler's favor; and among neighboring cities and towns Lowell was for and Cambridge against him, Quincy, for and Newton against him; and so it went.

He hoped of course to carry the convention. It was believed on the night before the regular session (so the Springfield *Republican* reports) that there were 350 dele-

[1] *Advertiser*, Aug. 25, 1871.

[2] Aug. 30 and Sept. 4, 1871.

[3] *Post*, Sept. 21 and 23, 1871.

gates for Washburn, 125 for Rice, 125 for Loring and 500 for Butler. Butler's first effort was to bring about a discussion of credentials. In this he failed. The convention voted to admit every delegate who bore a certificate from the chairman and secretary of a meeting regularly called and held at the place and hour named in the call, and to throw out contestants as bolters. This, according to the reporter of the *Republican*,[1] let in the delegates chosen by majorities made up of Labor Reformers, Democrats and non-residents; in short it gave Butler the benefit of his bold captures of Republican meetings by non-Republicans. But this vote prevented a discussion of credentials in open convention and left the decision to the committee. By the vote it was evident that he could not swing the convention, whereupon he ceased his aggressive policy. The regulars, however, did not relax their vigilance. Both Rice and Loring refused to be candidates for the nomination. There could thus be no division in the regular vote through which Butler might obtain the nomination. The Rice delegates and most of the Loring men voted for Washburn. Of the votes cast, Washburn received 643 and Butler 464.

When it was thus evident that the party leaders had outgeneralled Butler, he did not bolt, as might have been expected, but stood by the action of the convention.

In the words of the partisan press, " He marched over the state with the stride and voice of a braggart." [2] Yet he had nevertheless voiced the growing dissatisfaction with the administration in terms of local issues which had appealed to the interest of the people, and in spite of party organization and the opposition of the press, had won for himself a goodly minority. It was with great relief that the regular Republicans greeted the news of his defeat.

[1] Sept. 27, 1871.
[2] *Advertiser*, Sept. 29, 1871.

The Butler episode of 1873 was similar to that of 1871. Again local issues were raised, and prohibition was given especial prominence. Again, by his own labors in speech-making and by the excellent organization of his campaign, he won many delegates and hoped to carry the convention. But when he talked of reform, his opponents spoke of the "salary grab" which he had supported; when he talked of prohibition, they pointed to the saloon-keepers in his ranks. The regulars feared his power and held anti-Butler meetings, while the Democrats distrusted him because of his deflection to the Republican party during the war; the *Post* had a personal grievance against him,[1] and the newspapers generally were opposed to him. The *Republican*, indeed, said, " His strength is merely in quarters totally unaffected by newspaper articles." [2]

He approached the convention, nevertheless, with apparent assurance. On the day preceding the sitting of the convention the Butlerites posted a bulletin claiming 527 delegates as opposed, to 506 for Washburn, 70 not reported. At the same hour and place the bulletin of the regulars claimed 602 as opposed, to 440 for Butler, 40 in doubt and 26 not reported.[3] In the convention Butler again tested his strength in the attempt to have credentials discussed generally. He presented a resolution that Henry M. Green of Franklin, who had said if Butler was nominated he would bolt from the convention, should be debarred from taking part in the proceedings. The resolution, novel in substance as it was, did provoke consider-

[1] According to the Springfield *Republican* (Aug. 11, 1873), the *Post* held Butler largely responsible for the widening of the street near the U. S. Post-Office which would compel the *Post* to give up its building and find new quarters.

[2] July 17, 1873.

[3] Springfield *Republican*, Sept. 10, 1873.

able discussion before the regulars moved to refer it to the committee on credentials. That motion was carried by 584 yeas (from Washburn delegates), and 539 noes (Butler votes). Again he evidently could not carry the convention; but he did not give up immediately. It was objected by a Butler delegate that there were not 1123 men in convention, whereupon William M. Rice, a Washburn delegate, moved that voting should be done by counties. This motion was carried by 586 yeas to 406 noes. Butler at first determined to have the vote on the motion to refer to committee verified, but in the evening withdrew his motion to that effect. He was convinced by this time that the majority of the delegates were in favor of Washburn, and he therefore withdrew his candidacy.[1]

The election following, like that of 1871, was a party victory on general principles. When the internal conflict was over the Republican party, confident of its usual success, temporized with current issues in vague resolutions. Its main planks were party acknowledgment and general national topics. Then for the twelfth year the Republicans held the power in Massachusetts, and held it on national issues. But the majority in both 1871 and 1873 was much smaller than in the presidential year,—evidence of a growing dissatisfaction and a changing of issues. There was no longer any necessity to support the Republican party in order to attain military victory, nor, in the eyes of a growing number, was such support longer requisite for the guardianship of the victory already attained. The Republican party, persisting in its platform of "greater questions of national policy," remained in power, but by a vote of only 54 per cent.

In 1874 it lost even this small majority. The local topics

[1] Springfield *Republican*, and *Advertiser*, Sept. 11, 1873.

which had come to the front since the close of the war,—
labor, temperance, woman suffrage,—the party had endeavored to ignore, but had been forced to notice. Its organization and strength had been able to withstand the attempt
of Butler to secure his own supremacy through championing all the popular issues at once; but in 1874 general national topics were dull, Butler was quiet and the temperance issue, unhampered by other reforms and unaffected
by the personal standing of a conspicuous champion, proved
itself of sufficient concern to the people of the state to
subordinate all other issues and secure in the vote for governor an expression of opinion on this topic alone. This
vote, which defeated prohibition, discredited the Republican
candidate for governor.

Lieutenant-governor Talbot had succeeded to the gover-
norship on April 30, 1874, when Governor Washburn resigned to become senator. In June he vetoed two measures
of the legislature to abolish the state constabulary, and also
" an act regulating the sale of spirituous or intoxicating
liquors " which was to do away with the prohibitory law.
This check on legislative action was widely denounced. As
the campaign approached, in consequence, Governor Talbot
wrote a letter saying that he considered the Republican
party necessary to the country, and that therefore it had
better nominate some candidate whose views on the temperance question should not lessen the harmony within the
party.[1]

The convention, however, with a large prohibitionist con-
stituency, was loyal to its governor. Thus so far as Talbot
was concerned there was an alliance between the Prohibitionists and the Republicans. Such an alliance with local

[1] Letter to the Republican state committee; *Am. Annual Cyclop.*, 1875,
p. 477.

propaganda was quite contrary to the previous consistent practice of the party, and brought temporary defeat. There had, to be sure, been murmured and outspoken dissatisfaction with the state government (other than that voiced by Butler) for some time. There was a growing conviction that it had been in the same hands long enough. There was dissatisfaction with affairs at Washington, and one means of expressing that dissatisfaction was to discredit the party within the state. There was very strong disgust with the partial enforcement of the prohibition law, and with the consequent demoralizing effect of such lawlessness. And finally, there was rage on the part of many that the " no " of one man should block the will of the legislature for change in this matter. All these factors were at work, and when the Republican party braced itself against the next definite grievance, the prohibitory law, then that party was destined to defeat.

Gaston, the Democratic candidate for governor, carried all but four districts, Worcester and the three around Boston, but the other executive officers were Republican with their customary majorities. In the senate there were 24 Republicans, 15 Democrats, and 1 Independent, while there were in the house 155 Republicans, 79 Democrats and 6 Independents, thus giving the senate a majority of 8 Republicans and the house a majority of 70. This legislative majority favored a modification of the liquor laws, so that we might conclude that the decision was not so much against the Republican party as it was against the alliance between Republicans and Prohibitionists. But the congressional elections show increasing dissatisfaction with the administration of the dominant party: there were five Republican, four Democratic and two Independent congressmen.[1]

[1] *Advertiser* and *Post*, Nov. 4, 1874; and *Am. Annual Cyclop.*, 1874, p. 523.

This diminution of the Republican majority continued after 1874, but in slighter measure: one anti-Republican congressman was elected in each of the next three congressional elections, and in 1882 four were chosen. In 1876 the people supported Hayes, but with a less firm majority than any president had received in twenty years, while Charles Francis Adams, the Democratic nominee for governor, was defeated by a very narrow margin. At the same time, the legislature was still held by a staunch Republican majority: there were 33 Republicans to 7 Democrats in the senate, and 178 to 62 in the house. By 1876 important local and new national issues had broken the solid Republican ranks and continued so to do until erstwhile regulars such as John Murray Forbes [1] followed Charles Francis Adams into the Democratic party.

With the rise and dominance of the Democratic party in Massachusetts we are not concerned. We have traced the course of political opinion in the state through the periods of the Civil War and the Reconstruction, and have seen that that opinion stood in general for two successive principles. The first of these, prevalent throughout the Civil War, was the support of the administration in the preservation of the Union, through emancipation, if need be, although emancipation was for the most part a subsidiary issue. The second principle, governing the period of the Reconstruction, was that of the support of the victorious party, which is to say the Republican party, in securing to the country union, nationality, and lasting democracy as the permanent fruits of victory. In neither period was there unanimity of opinion. In the war period there were critics and copperheads who worked against the administration; at the beginning of reconstruction days there were

[1] Forbes, *Letters and Recollections*, vol. ii, p. 142.

divergent theories. But both copperheads and theorists disappeared. The former gradually lost sympathy for the desperate and defeated cause. Of the latter some became tempered by interest in local issues; while the majority acquiesced in the theories of the party leaders, from what, at the time, appeared to be the necessity of the case. That necessity, as interpreted by the majority throughout the whole period, was the preservation of the Union, through the support of the administration to the accomplishment of military success, and through the establishment of the Constitution, by the party that had saved it, within the Southern states with amendments which should in the belief of Republican leaders, secure republicanism and democracy for the entire country. When in form at least that purpose appeared to be accomplished, the people of Massachusetts turned their attention to matters of administrative reform and to local interests.

APPENDIX II

THE PRESS OF MASSACHUSETTS DURING THE SIXTIES

THE purpose of this sketch is to describe the various newspapers quoted in the monograph, to state the politics and estimate the influence of each, as well as to show why these particular papers were selected as adequate evidence of the opinion of the whole state. Concerning the last point it is obvious that the task of reading all the Massachusetts dailies and weeklies of the Civil War and Reconstruction periods would be long and repetitious and not altogether necessary, for, since newspapers are not all individual in their views but are generally party organs, it is possible to group the numerous files in the Boston Public Library and the American Antiquarian Society in such a way that a few representative sheets will give an adequate estimate of the opinions of the press. And since leading papers are widely read and frequently quoted, it is possible to read the leading papers of each faction, and thus ascertain the views of and within the various parties. Yet it must always be remembered that a newspaper may express the view of a faction and not express the view of the people; for editors often tried to mold public sentiment instead of expressing it, or they talked loud and long to direct opinion into channels they thought wise or profitable. On the other hand, where there was but one newspaper in a community, as in many small cities and towns, that newspaper was not so strongly partisan as the Boston publications. It is true, too, that such a paper often shows the consensus of opinion of its locality; for, if it did not at first express what the people already thought, the people soon thought what the paper persistently reiterated. Therefore, in the following description, an effort will be made to show not only the politics of the papers consulted, but, whenever possible, the extent to which they expressed or molded public opinion.

Among the more eminent formulators of opinion, the beacon lights of their communities were notably the Newburyport *Herald*, the Worcester *Spy*, and the Springfield *Republican*.[1] Naturally the smaller local papers followed the lead of nearby prominent dailies; when a prominent daily is read, therefore, the point of view presented to the people of its section of Massachusetts is easily ascertained. Nevertheless a few of the local weekly papers were well edited and had an influence similar to that of the more famous dailies. The Hampshire *Gazette*, for example, although it generally followed the lead of the Springfield *Republican,* must be ranked with its leader because its influence was similar; the *Gazette* was in fact held by its readers to be " law and gospel ".[2] And in all probability the Essex County *Mercury* was to the rural districts around Salem what the *Gazette* was to the Hadleys.

Of these notable formulators of public opinion, the Newburyport *Herald* was conservative, the Worcester *Spy* radical and the Springfield *Republican* judicious and the champion of administration policies. The first had been a Whig paper, and although its position was that " the union of these states should be maintained ",[3] yet it opposed all abolitionist agita-

---

[1] Gladden, *Recollections*, pp. 242-245, explains that the method by which the Springfield *Republican* obtained and kept such remarkable hold on the towns of western Massachusetts was the column of local items. Through it the paper contained something of immediate interest to each family,—a policy first inaugurated by the Hampshire *Gazette*.

[2] Godwin, *Life of Bryant*, vol. i, p. 128. A letter of Bryant describes the influence of the *Gazette* at an earlier time. The description was true of the sixties, judging from the testimony of contemporaries. "Let the 'Hampshire *Gazette*' only give the word," Bryant writes, "which, by the by, it copies from some leading Federalist paper, and every Federalist in the country has his cue, everybody knows what to think."

[3] Newburyport *Herald*, April 8, 1861; also testimony of Rev. John R. Thurston, resident of Newburyport in the sixties.

tion and was not pleased with the Emancipation Proclamation. The city of its publication, a seaport, profited from Southern trade; and, because of the community's commercial interests, the *Herald* was loath to see the institution of the South disturbed.

On the other hand the *Spy*, " the infallible sheet " of Worcester County, was strongly anti-slavery: in 1862, for example it was anxious for emancipation and urged that policy while its neighbor, the Springfield *Republican*, held back, awaiting the action of the administration. Indeed, the Boston *Courier* accused the *Spy*, because of its anti-slavery tendency, of being abolitionist, and when it opposed the compromise measures of 1861 classed it with the New Bedford *Standard*, the Salem *Gazette*, the Fall River *News*, and the Boston *Traveller*, all of which it said were as much Garrisonian as the *Liberator*.[1] In the early part of the war the columns of the *Spy* were filled with reports of battles and the conditions of the soldiers; financial problems incident to the war were described, not discussed. Thus, excluding its policy as to emancipation, it usually gave the facts and left the people to form their own opinions concerning the policy of the administration. After the war the main idea of the *Spy* was impartial suffrage; it tolerated various laws passed by Congress, but held that they were inadequate; it was vehement in its opposition to Johnson and disgruntled that he was not convicted. Until this disappointment, however, the *Spy's* news and descriptions of the progress of reconstruction continued to be very complete and satisfactory.

The last named prominent daily, the Springfield *Republican,* took the middle ground and stood squarely by the administration; it defended every action and would forestall any independent criticism of the government. Its attitude toward any possible action of the president for emancipation is only illustrative of its whole policy. In this connection it declared its purpose to stand by him and his chosen generals, and,

[1] *Courier*, Feb. 21, Nov. 19, 1861.

whether or not it approved of all he did, to do nothing
to weaken his hands, or to destroy the faith of the people in
him.[1]   And thus throughout the war, although the *Republican*
was conservative, it was, above all else, the administration
paper.[2]   Nevertheless it was liberal: it allowed its correspondents to say what they believed even though their views
did not coincide with the policy of the editors.   This is true,
especially, of the letters of Warrington the Boston correspondent, who was more aggressive in his desire for emancipation
than were Samuel Bowles and his associates.[3]   But in spite
of this liberality the paper exerted its greatest influence
through its editorials, which, did we not know the policy of
the paper, would almost appear to have been prophetic in their
judgment.   It manifested the same farsightedness during reconstruction times.   It was among the earliest to recognize
the wisdom of Andrew's valedictory suggestions; it believed
in democracy and therefore in universal suffrage; yet it also
believed in amnesty and in the rebuilding of the South by its
natural leaders.   In the seventies, however, it resented the
corruption and the domination of the Republicans, and, therefore, it supported the reaction against the party.   Unquestionably throughout the period, whether in loyalty or later opposition, the *Republican* always spoke the sentiment of the
more discreet Republicans.[4]

[1] Springfield *Republican*, July 26, 1862.

[2] When Samuel Bowles was in Europe in 1862, and later when he was
in California, the paper was under the direction of Dr. Holland.   Then
it swerved a little in its general policy, *e. g.*, in 1862 it supported the
anti-administration People's party.   But on the return of Bowles it
again championed the administration.   *Cf.* Merriam, *Life of Bowles*,
vol. i, pp. 357-358.

[3] Warrington was William S. Robinson, a member of the Bird Club.   He
wrote for the *Atlas and the Bee*, and for the *Commonwealth*, because in
them he could express his anti-slavery beliefs.   Other Boston papers
would not accept his articles.—*"Warrington" Pen Portraits*, p. 94.
Merriam (*Life of Bowles*, vol. i, p. 388) characterizes him as the
cayenne pepper of the *Republican* salad in the years between the birth
of the Republican party and the Greeley revolt.

[4] Even the *Courier* testifies to this, Aug. 30, 1861.

Among the representative papers of Boston, those most often quoted were the *Traveller, Courier, Journal, Post* and *Advertiser*.

The first named is said to have been " the *Transcript* of the sixties ", a household necessity, while the *Journal* was essentially the organ of news, giving full telegraphic reports of congressional and legislative proceedings, and boasting as its Washington correspondent Ben: Perley Poore. It was also conspicuous as the two-cent sheet when all others were three cents, and it probably and perhaps consequently had the largest circulation. The third Republican publication of this Boston group and perhaps the most important was the *Advertiser*. It, like the *Traveller*, was a household necessity, but it was more; it was a political necessity as well. A decade earlier, like the Newburyport *Herald*, it had been a Whig paper and, like the *Herald*, it remained conservative, though not to the same degree as the sheet of the lesser town; the *Advertiser* was, on the contrary, wholeheartedly Republican. The esteem in which it was held and the influence it exerted are constantly in evidence. It is always the paper mentioned by the correspondents of Andrew, Forbes, Sumner and Lawrence; it is described by contemporaries as " reliable ", by rivals as " respectable ",[1] and by friends affectionately named the " Tiser ".[2] Moreover the prominent directors of opinion wrote for it under frequently recurring pen names. " Audax " or " Economist," for example, was John Murray Forbes, " Americanus " was Theophilus Parsons,[3] and " N " was C. E. Norton. In consequence of these contributions the New England Loyal Publication Society quoted largely from

[1] *E. g.,* Courier, Mar. 24, 1863.

[2] *E. g.,* Forbes, *Letters (Supplementary)*, vol. ii, p. 196, to C. E. Norton, Dec. 31, 1863.

[3] *Sumner MSS*, from Theophilus Parsons, Dec. 23, 1864. Also from George Bemis, Jan. 13, 1863, we learn " Jus " was C. F. Blake; and from Theophilus Parsons, Feb. 1, 1865, that " Privaticus " was Robert C. Winthrop.

articles of the *Advertiser*, thus saving labor and, at the same extending the influence of that paper.

The two other prominent Boston dailies, the *Post* and the *Courier*, were anti-Republican, anti-administration, anti-war and sometimes anti-Union. The *Post*,[1] according to the *Spy*, was the " Boston organ of official Democracy ".[2] It also represented the commercial interest that would conciliate the South because a quarrel with that section of the country might deprive New England of her customers; it was for the same reason opposed to any interference with the institution of slavery; it supported Breckinridge in 1860, partly because it had quarrelled with Douglas on the Kansas issues, and partly because Breckinridge was the candidate of the South. In general it stood for the Union during the war, and for immediate restoration as soon as the war was over. It had been consistently Democratic; on the other hand the *Courier*, like the *Advertiser* and the Newburyport *Herald*, had earlier been a Whig paper, and in January, 1860, was favorable to the Democrats,[3] but under the leadership of George Lunt and George Hillard it became the organ of the Constitutional Union party. It took as its motto, " The Union, the Constitution, the Enforcement of the Laws." On March 20, 1860, it declared that there ought to be a party organized " with the express purpose in view of putting an end to anti-slavery agitation—that acknowledged source of vast political, economical and social evils and absolute bane of our national welfare." Thus it is easy to understand why the *Liberator*

---

[1] " The circulation of the Boston *Post* is nearly double that of any other 3-cent commercial paper in Boston."—From head of editorial column, March, 1860. This statement must stand for whatever it may mean on the surface. An effort was made to get newspaper statistics, but none were available; the above statement, therefore, like that concerning the circulation of the *Journal* (*supra*, p. 205), is given for its face value.

[2] Worcester *Spy*, April 2, 1860.

[3] Coleman, *Life of Crittenden*, vol. ii, p. 183. Letter from Amos A. Lawrence, Jan. 6, 1860.

spoke of it as "a villainous sheet." [1] In July, 1860, the New York *Tribune* had said that among the conservative journals the *Courier* was "the ablest"; but before its decease in December, 1864, it was very poorly conducted and deserved a measure of George Livermore's characterization, "that infamous reservoir of treason, mendacity and scurrility." [2]

Besides the well established papers [3] which molded opinion and expressed party views, there were in Boston special campaign sheets,[4] which expressed the views and supported the policy of Governor Andrew and the Bird Club; [5] they

[1] *Liberator*, Dec. 7, 1860.

[2] *Sumner MSS*, Jan. 12, 1864. Livermore states that George Hillard was no longer connected with the paper. James Freeman Clarke's characterization of it is amusing: "People have croaked at every advance of the human race. . . . I look upon the Boston *Courier* as a kind of marsh which has been providentially provided for these people, where they can sit and croak to each other in a sort of frog concert of mutual condolence." Sermon: April 2, 1863.

[3] The New York *Tribune* should also be taken into account, for, though not belonging to Massachusetts, it was widely read, frequently quoted and implicitly believed. Miss Ann Page and Captain Comey (2d Mass.), of Danvers, for example, say that the New York *Tribune* was a great factor in molding opinion in their neighborhood. Gladden, *Recollections*, p. 173, says it was the "Republican Bible". No statistics are available as to the number of its subscribers, but on Dec. 8, 1859, the *Courier*, in praise of the *Journal*, said it exceeded the *Tribune* by 5,000 copies. Evidently the *Tribune* had a strong following if it was success to surpass it.

[4] "*Warrington*" *Pen Portraits*, pp. 93-94. Mrs. Robinson describes these special papers. She attributes much importance to their influence.

[5] Sanborn, *Life of Howe*, p. 252, note 1: "The Bird Club originated about 1850 in the dining together at George Young's Hotel in Boston of a few of the political anti-slavery men, who, like Francis William Bird of Walpole, were active in elections and campaigns. By 1856, when the Kansas troubles came on, it had become a large and powerful body of men, with no definite organization, who looked upon Mr. Bird as their friend, and brought other friends to sit at his weekly clubtable. At one time perhaps one hundred men were members of this Round Table, which met weekly at Young's or Parker's to dine

stood, as no commercial paper would have dared stand, for an aggressive Republicanism. For example, the *Tocsin* first appeared, on February 1, 1861, with the motto, "No more compromise with slavery"; the six numbers that were published contained articles by Elizur Wright, F. W. Bird, F. B. Sanborn and W. S. Robinson, all members of the Bird Club, against the repeal of the Personal Liberty Bill, against the Virginia Peace Conference, and in favor of radical anti-slavery measures.[1] Another instance of these campaign publications is the *Weekly Commonwealth*, which was first projected by the Emancipation League.[2] In 1862 it was supported largely by George L. Stearns and edited by F. B. Sanborn[3] for the purpose of reëlecting Charles Sumner; it advocated emancipation, the enlistment of colored soldiers and other radical anti-slavery measures. The *Commonwealth* was longer-lived than the *Tocsin*, and during reconstruction times its general principle was the support of Congress, right or

together. With the election of Governor Andrew in 1860, they took charge of the State Government of Massachusetts, and controlled it for a dozen years, or until 1873." Edward L. Pierce, however, says the first company was of Free-Soilers in 1853, that in 1857 there was a division into Banks and Birdmen, and that again in 1872 there was a second division because Bird opposed Grant's re-election. F. B. Sanborn, in reminiscence, said that in 1862-1863 "it was no unusual thing to see at the dinner-table on Saturdays the two Senators, Sumner and Wilson, Gov. Andrew, half a dozen Congressmen, with Dr. Howe, Mr. Bird, George L. Stearns, and many more of the radical Republicans of New England." Similarly introduction to "*Warrington*" *Pen Portraits*. On the occasion of the last meeting of the club various newspapers had sketches of its work and influence, *e. g.*, Boston *Herald*, April 27, 1901, and Springfield *Weekly Republican*, May 3, 1901.

[1] *Sumner MSS*, from W. S. Robinson, Feb. 6, 1861: "I send you a second number of the *Tocsin*, with which Howe, Stearns, Bird, J. M. Stone, Elizur Wright and I are trying to keep up the spirit of the Legislature." Also, "*Warrington*" *Pen Portraits*, p. 93.

[2] *Cf. supra*, ch. iv.

[3] Testimony of F. B. Sanborn.

wrong. A third special sheet was the *Atlas and Bee*.[1]
Founded by printers in 1842 in support of the Know-Nothings,
it was the only political anti-slavery paper in Boston [2] during
1860 and to July, 1861. It alone, of all the Boston daily
papers, uttered " hearty fitting rebuke " to the pro-slavery
mob in Boston, December 3, 1861. On June 24, 1861, it declared its position as follows: " We believe that adjustments,
compromises, settlements, bargains, are futile and useless and
impossible. The present is a struggle for life; it is a war of
systems; liberty or slavery; republicanism or despotism. . . .
We are pledged to support the most vigorous war measures
of Congress and the President." All these campaign papers
undoubtedly had influence unmeasured by their circulation,
for mention of their position is frequently found in the well
established dailies.

Classed with the special sheets because of its influence
through quotation may come the work of the New England
Loyal Publication Society. This society was launched by
John Murray Forbes.[3] He perceived that Lincoln would advance only so far and so fast as he was sure public sentiment
would support him; Forbes and his colleagues, therefore,
determined to formulate an opinion that would make it possible for Lincoln to advance.[4] Through its broadsides the

---

[1] The *Atlas and Bee* varied its title: *Atlas and Daily Bee*, Jan., 1860–
May 16, 1860; *Daily Atlas and Bee*, May 16, 1860–June 24, 1861; *Boston
Daily Atlas*, June 24, 1861–July 8, 1861. It was discontinued altogether
on July 8, 1861.

[2] *"Warrington" Pen Portraits*, p. 94; Springfield *Republican*, July
31, 1861.

[3] Forbes, *Recollections*, vol. ix, p. 328; also *cf. supra*, ch. v.

[4] " I wish you could elaborate the above idea about recruiting our
army—Stanton opposes it, so we must *make* public opinion."—Post-
script of a letter to C. E. Norton, Dec. 29, 1863, MS in *New England
Loyal Publication Society Collection;* similarly Forbes, *Letters (Supplementary)*, vol. ii, p. 64, to Madame De Tocqueville, Feb. 6, 1863.
Pearson, Forbes, pp. 135-7, gives a sketch of the work and influence
of the society.

Society advocated Union primarily, emancipation as a military necessity, vigorous prosecution of the war, enlistment of colored soldiers, universal suffrage and other policies which in time were realized.

Pamphlets also may be grouped with special publications. There were a few that favored secession and opposed the policies of the administration, but the majority were published with a purpose like that of the Loyal Publication Society. The speeches of senators and representatives were published in pamphlet form when it was thought that they would help to formulate opinion. It cannot be denied that the supporters of the war were inspired with missionary zeal and left no stone unturned in their endeavor to achieve their ideal.[1]

Besides the publications already discussed, there were religious periodicals which must be taken into account. The New York *Independent* was widely read in Massachusetts. The *Congregationalist* was the publication of the Congregational Church, which was in the majority in Massachusetts. These weeklies were as anti-slavery in sentiment as were the special campaigners. Not all the religious papers were of this tone, however, for the Boston *Pilot,* an ably conducted Catholic newspaper, was pro-slavery and Democratic.[2]

And finally standing by itself, was the *Liberator,* implicitly trusted by some and violently hated by others. It was the mouthpiece of extreme abolitionists. It was early opposed

[1] A letter from J. M. Forbes to C. E. Norton (June 28, 1864) illustrates: " In clearing up old scores I find a note from you asking me if I know the character of Frank Blair's bill for recruiting in the Rebel states. Didn't I spend a month at that sink of iniquity, Washington, dinging it into Senator's ears, and didn't Wilson confess that by dint of forcing and bringing the New York and Philadelphia Leagues to bear, we got the Senate from ⅔ against it to a majority for it, whenever it can fairly be got up?—but there was the rub. I now hand you a copy of the bill which I hope to see pass as an amendment to the enrollment bill, and if so we must fire a broadside into Stanton and force him to carry out the will of Congress." Forbes, *Letters (Supplementary),* vol. ii, p. 268.

[2] *Cf. supra,* ch. iv.

to the government. Its doctrine was " No union with slave-
holders "; its motto, " The Constitution is a Covenant with
Death and an Agreement with Hell," was later (December,
1861), changed to " Proclaim Liberty throughout all the Land,
to all the Inhabitants thereof ". With the adoption of the
Thirteenth Amendment William Lloyd Garrison believed his
work was done [1] and the paper was discontinued.

These newspapers have been selected as representative.
While they are but a portion of those on file, it is possible
to obtain from them an adequate idea of the political opinion
of Massachusetts as found in the press.

[1] The Newburyport *Herald*, April 24, 1863, paid the following tribute
to William Lloyd Garrison: " William Lloyd Garrison is now the old-
est editor in Boston, counting professional life alone; he is also the
most successful. There is not an editor in Boston or the world who
has been the means of accomplishing as great a revolution in public
sentiment and public action as he. Of the anti-slavery movement which
has culminated in this mighty civil war he can say — ' Solitary and
alone I set this ball in motion.' People tell of the influence of the
Tribune, of Charles Sumner, of political and religious anti-slavery
societies; but of all these Lloyd Garrison was the author—the father.
He first declared for immediate and unconditional emancipation. . . .
We do not agree with him, but think to do him no more than justice."
This and similar statements have been believed. As tribute it has
fallen into the error of exaggerated statement. William Lloyd Garrison undoubtedly was a courageous and able editor, but that he accomplished a revolution in public sentiment and public action is not true.
That was accomplished by the necessities of the times, as has been
shown, *supra*, ch. iv.

APPENDIX III

BIBLIOGRAPHICAL NOTE

Besides the newspaper records, noted in Appendix ii,[1] contemporaneous opinion may be found in correspondence, published and unpublished, in pamphlets, in broadsides, in magazines and in literary works.

MANUSCRIPTS

A number of collections of manuscripts are of high importance:

The official correspondence of Governor John A. Andrew is in the executive offices at the State House, Boston. (His daughter, Miss Edith Andrews, has his personal correspondence, but owing to Miss Andrew's ill health these papers are not available. Professor Henry Greenleaf Pearson has consulted them and embodied the more important in his *Life of John A. Andrew*.)

The Charles Sumner papers, which are in the Harvard University Library, comprise letters received: they include many from John A. Andrew, John Murray Forbes, George S. Boutwell, Richard Henry

[1] The newspapers might be listed here for convenience:

The *Atlas and Bee* (1844–1861).
The Boston *Daily Advertiser* (1813–).
The *Weekly Commonwealth* (1862–1895).
The Boston *Courier* (1824–1864).
The Hampshire *Gazette* (Weekly, 1787–, Daily, 1890–).
The Newburyport *Herald* (Daily, 1832–).
The Boston *Journal* (1833–).
The *Liberator* (Boston, 1831–1865).
The *Pilot* (Boston, 1829–).
The Boston *Post* (1831–).
The Springfield *Republican* (Weekly, 1824–, Daily, 1844–).
The Worcester *Spy* (Weekly, 1775–, Daily, 1845–, discontinued, 1904)
The Boston *Traveller* (1845–).
The Boston *Evening Transcript* (1830–).

212   [408

Dana, Jr., Edward Everett Hale, L. Maria Child, Wendell Phillips, John D. Baldwin and Edward L. Pierce.

The Harvard Archives contain the correspondence of its presidents, C. C. Felton (1860-1861) and A. P. Peabody, concerning the enlistment of Harvard students.

The *Reminiscences* and *Letters* of John Murray Forbes have been published privately for his descendants. The *Reminiscences* are in three volumes, as are the *Letters* (*Supplementary*). These six volumes have been edited by his daughter, Sarah Forbes Hughes (printed by George H. Ellis, Boston, 1902).

The Massachusetts Historical Society possesses the Winthrop, Bancroft and Schouler manuscripts, and is the custodian of the Amos A. Lawrence papers. The Lawrence collection is very complete, containing both letter presses and letters received. The Robert C. Winthrop papers are also extensive: they include letters received and copies of letters written to Judge John H. Clifford, and to John P. Kennedy of Baltimore. The letters to William Schouler, adjutant-general of Massachusetts (1861-1866) are of little importance to the present work. The George Bancroft papers include a number of letters from Massachusetts correspondents.

Abolition correspondence, the Weston and the Garrison manuscripts, are in the Boston Public Library. The Garrison collection is very complete.

The Eli Thayer papers are in the John Hay Library, Brown University.

The private papers of Edward Everett and Richard Henry Dana, Jr., are in the possession of the respective families but are not now accessible to the public.

PUBLISHED CORRESPONDENCE AND SPEECHES

The published correspondence and speeches are to be found, in part or entire, in journals, memoirs, biographies, etc. The opinions, comments, speeches, which the author found valuable were those of

Adams, Charles Francis, in Massachusetts Historical Society, *Proceedings*, Nov., 1911, pp. 76-148; extracts from his letters are contained in a biography by his son, Charles Francis Adams (American Statesmen Series). Boston, 1900.

Andrew, John A., extracts from whose letters are contained in the *Life of John A. Andrew* by Henry Greenleaf Pearson, ii vols. Boston, 1904.

Boutwell, George S., *Speeches and Papers relating to the Rebellion and the Overthrow of Slavery*. Boston, 1867.

Bowditch, Henry Ingersoll, The Life and Correspondence of, by his son Vincent Y. Bowditch, ii vols. Boston, 1902.

Bullock, Alexander Hamilton, *Addresses* delivered by. Boston, 1883.

Child, Lydia Maria, Letters of. Boston, 1883.

Curtis, Benjamin Robbins, whose speeches are contained in *A Memoir* edited by Benjamin R. Curtis, ii vols. Boston, 1879.

Dana, Jr., Richard Henry, extracts from whose letters are contained in a biography by Charles Francis Adams, ii vols. Boston, 1890.

Emerson, Ralph Waldo, *The Correspondence of Thomas Carlyle and Ralph Waldo Emerson,* edited by Charles Eliot Norton, ii vols., Boston, 1883. And *Journals of Ralph Waldo Emerson, 1820–1876,* edited by Edward Waldo Emerson and Waldo Emerson Forbes, x vols. (vols. ix and x). Boston, 1913.

Everett, Edward, *Orations and Speeches on Various Occasions,* iv vols. (vol. iv). Boston, 1868. Letters to and from Edward Everett are contained in the *Life of John J. Crittenden* by Mrs. Chapman Coleman, ii vols. Philadelphia, 1871. There is also a letter in a biography of William Cullen Bryant by Parke Goodwin. New York, 1883.

Forbes, John Murray, *Letters and Recollections,* edited by Sarah Forbes Hughes, ii vols. Boston, 1899.

Garrison, William Lloyd, whose letters and speeches are contained in a biography by his children, iv vols. (vol. iv). New York, 1889.

Gray, Asa, Letters of, edited by Jane Loring Gray, ii vols. Boston, 1893.

Holmes, Oliver Wendell, Life and Letters of, by John T. Morse, Jr., ii vols. Boston, 1896.

Howe, Samuel Gridley, Letters and Journals of, edited by Laura E. Richards, ii vols. Boston, 1909.

Lawrence, Amos A., extracts from whose letters are contained in a biography by his son William Lawrence. Boston, 1888. Letters to and from Amos A. Lawrence are also contained in the *Life of John J. Crittenden* by Mrs. Chapman Coleman, ii vols. Philadelphia, 1871.

Longfellow, Henry Wadsworth, extracts from whose journals and correspondence are published in a biography by Samuel Longfellow. Boston, 1886.

Lowell, Charles Russell, Life and Letters of, by Edward W. Emerson. Boston, 1907.

Lowell, James Russell, Letters of, edited by Charles Eliot Norton, ii vols. New York, 1894.

Morse, Charles F., *Letters written during the Civil War, 1861-1865.* Privately printed, 1898.

Motley, John Lothrop, *The Correspondence of,* edited by George William Curtis, ii vols. London, 1889.

Norton, Charles Eliot, *Letters of,* edited by his daughter Sara Norton and M. A. DeW. Howe, ii vols. Boston, 1913.

Phillips, Wendell, *Speeches, Lectures and Letters.* Boston, 1863.
Sumner, Charles, *Memoir and Letters of,* by Edward L. Pierce, iv vols.,
    Boston, 1893; and *Works of,* xii vols. (vols. v–ix), Boston, 1895.
Ticknor, George, Life, Letters and Journals of, ii vols. Boston, 1876.
Robinson, William S., *" Warrington" Pen Portraits,* edited by Mrs. W.
    S. Robinson. Boston, 1877.
Whittier, John Greenleaf, Life and Letters of, by Samuel T. Pickard,
    ii vols. or vols. x and xi of *Works of Whittier.* Boston, 1894.
Winthrop, Robert C., *Addresses and Speeches,* 1852-1867, ii vols. Bos-
    ton, 1867.

PAMPHLETS

The pamphlets are numerous. There are two special collections in the Boston Public Library: the *American Anti-
slavery Tract,* 1860-1862, published in Boston by R. F. Wall-
cutt, in New York by the American Antislavery Society; and
the *Loyal Publication Society Pamphlets,* nos. 1-44, (Feb. 1,
1863—Feb. 1, 1864), New York: Loyal Publication Society,
1864. Besides these special collections both the Boston Public Library and the State Library have collections of separate
pamphlets. These comprise many sermons dealing with the
momentous questions of the hour, reprints of congressional
speeches, reprints of important articles from the *North American Review* and the *Atlantic Monthly,* and almost innumer-
able separate pamphlets. These last are the most valuable and
have been frequently quoted and frequently noted throughout this monograph.

BROADSIDES

Broadsides were especially valuable, chiefly the *Publications
of the Loyal Publication Society, 1862-1868.* There are two
collections of these publications: the more complete one is in
the Boston Public Library, the other is in the Rooms of the
Massachusetts Historical Society. Among the broadsides are
a few manuscript letters concerning the publications; there are
also notes concerning authorship.

The Boston Public Library also possesses numerous separate
broadsides: proclamations, general orders, poems, cartoons,

and sheets similar to those of the New England Loyal Publication Society.

Miss Eva Thayer, of Worcester, has two broadsides published by the Central Republican Club of Worcester in 1860.

MAGAZINES AND LITERARY WORKS

The magazines and literary works may be classed together, for the articles that appeared in the *North American Review* (vols. xcii-cx), the *Atlantic Monthly* (vols. vi-xxiii) and Littell's *Living Age* (vols. lxvi-civ), were frequently included in the collected works of their authors in later years. Obviously the opinion of the literary group *par excellence* — of Emerson, of Holmes, of Longfellow, of Lowell, of Whittier, expressed either in poetry or prose, is always available in their collected works.

DOCUMENTS

The documentary evidence of public opinion is found in Massachusetts Public Documents as follows:

Acts and Resolves passed by the General Court of Massachusetts in the years 1861-1874.

Legislative Documents of the Senate, 1860-1874.

Legislative Documents of the House, 1861-1874.

Journals of the Senate, 1861-1874. Those from 1861-1867 are in manuscript.

Journals of the House, 1861-1874. Those from 1861-1863 are in manuscript.

Addresses of the Governors are collected and bound together in the Massachusetts State Library.

BIOGRAPHIES, REMINISCENCES AND SECONDARY WORKS

Biographies, reminiscences and secondary works gave many suggestions and sometimes valuable data. The most useful were the following:

Adams, Charles Francis, 1835-1915; An Autobiography. Boston, 1916.
Adams, Charles Francis, *Charles Francis Adams* (American Statesmen Series). Boston, 1900.
———, *Richard Henry Dana, Jr.*, ii vols. Boston, 1890.

Austin, George Lowell, *The Life and Times of Wendell Phillips.* Boston, 1888.

Boutwell, George S., *Reminiscences of Sixty Years.* New York, 1902.

Bowen, James L., *Massachusetts in the War, 1861-1865.* Springfield, Mass., 1889.

Bowditch, Henry Ingersoll, Life and Correspondence of, by his son Vincent Y. Bowditch, ii vols. Boston, 1902.

Brown, Albert G., *Sketch of the Official Life of John A. Andrew.* New York, 1868.

Bridge, Horatio, *Personal Recollections of Nathaniel Hawthorne.* New York, 1893.

Butler, Benjamin Franklin, *Autobiography and Personal Reminiscences.* Boston, 1892.

Cabot, James Elliot, *A Memoir of Ralph Waldo Emerson,* ii vols. (or vols. xiii and xiv in the Standard Library Edition of Emerson's *Works*). Boston, 1887.

Carpenter, George Rice, *John Greenleaf Whittier* (American Men of Letters Series). Boston, 1903.

Chandler, Peleg W., *Memoir of Governor Andrew* (with Valedictory). Boston, 1880.

Chittenden, L. E., *A Report of the Debates and Proceedings in the Secret Sessions of the Conference Proposing Amendments to the Constitution of the United States.* New York, 1864.

Conway, Moncure D., *Life of Nathaniel Hawthorne.* London, 1891.

Cooke, George Willis, *Ralph Waldo Emerson.* Boston, 1882.

Curtis, Benjamin Robbins, *A Memoir,* edited by Benjamin R. Curtis, ii vols. Boston, 1879.

Curtis, George Ticknor, *Life of James Buchanan,* ii vols. New York, 1883.

Dunning, William A., *Essays on the Civil War and Reconstruction.* New York, 1910.

Forbes, John Murray, Letters and Recollections of, edited by Sarah Forbes Hughes, ii vols. Boston, 1899.

Forbes, John Murray, *A Sketch,* reprinted from the *Atantic Monthly,* Sept., 1899.

Forbes, Robert B., *Personal Reminiscences.* Boston, 1878.

Forney, John W., *Anecdotes of Public Men,* ii vols. New York, 1873.

Fite, Emerson David, *The Presidential Campaign of 1860.* New York, 1911.

Garrison, William Lloyd, told by his children, iv vols. New York, 1889.

Gladden, Washington, *Recollections.* Boston, 1909.

Gould, Alice Bache, *Louis Agassiz* (The Beacon Biographies). Boston, 1901.

Greenslet, Ferris, *Thomas Bailey Aldrich.* Boston, 1908.

——, *James Russell Lowell.* Boston, 1905.

Halstead, Murat, *Caucuses of 1860; A History of the National Polit-ical Conventions.* Columbus, 1860.

Hale, Edward Everett, *James Russell Lowell and his Friends.* Boston, 1899.

Haynes, George H., *Charles Sumner* (American Crisis Biographies). Philadelphia, 1909.

Headley, P. C., *Massachusetts in the Rebellion.* Boston, 1866.

Higginson, Thomas Wentworth, *Cheerful Yesterdays.* Boston, 1898.

Hoar, George F., *Autobiography of Seventy Years,* ii vols. New York, 1903.

Holmes, Oliver Wendell, *Ralph Waldo Emerson* (American Men of Letters Series). Boston, 1884.

——, *John Lothrop Motley, A Memoir.* Boston, 1881.

Johnson, Oliver, *William Lloyd Garrison.* Boston, 1880.

Kennedy, William Sloane, *Oliver Wendell Holmes.* Boston, 1883.

——, *John Greenleaf Whittier.* Boston, 1903.

Lincoln, Abraham, Memorial of. Boston, 1865.

Lanman, Charles, *Biographical Annals of the Civil Government of the United States.* Washington, 1876.

Lawrence, William, *Life of Amos A. Lawrence.* Boston, 1888.

Longfellow, Samuel, *Life of Henry Wadsworth Longfellow,* vols. xii to xiv of the *Works of Longfellow.* Boston, 1886.

Lunt, George, *The Origin of the Late War.* New York, 1886.

McCulloch, Hugh, *Men and Measures of Half a Century.* New York, 1888.

McPherson, Edward, *The Political History of the United States of America during the Great Rebellion.* Washington, 1865.

——, *The Political History of the United States of America during the Period of Reconstruction.* Washington, 1871.

Merriam, George S., *The Life and Times of Samuel Bowles,* ii vols. New York, 1885.

Morse, Jr., John T., *Life and Letters of Oliver Wendell Holmes,* ii vols. Boston, 1896.

Pearson, John Greenleaf, *Life of John A. Andrew.* ii vols. Boston, 1904.

——, *An American Railroad Builder.* Boston, 1911.

Oil on the Waters. Boston: J. E. Tilton & Co., 1867.

Poore, Ben Perley, *The Political Register and Congressional Direc-tory, 1776-1878.* Boston, 1878.

——, *Reminiscences of Sixty Years,* ii vols. Philadelphia, 1886.

Picard, Samuel T., *Life and Letters of John Greenleaf Whittier,* vols. ix and x of the *Works of Whittier.* Boston, 1894.

Pierce, Edward L., *Memoir and Letters of Charles Sumner,* iv vols. Boston, 1893.

Tribute of the Massachusetts Historical Society to the Memory of Josiah Quincy, *Proceedings*, Series i, vól. vii. Boston, 1864.

Rhodes, James Ford, *History of the United States from the Compromise of 1850*, vii vols. New York, 1893-1906.

Sanborn, F. B., *Dr. S. G. Howe—Philanthropist*. New York, 1891.

Scudder, Horace Elisha, *James Russell Lowell*, ii vols. Boston, 1901.

Sears, Lorenzo, *Wendell Phillips*. New York, 1909.

Schouler, William, *A History of Massachusetts in the Civil War*, ii vols. Boston, 1868-1871.

Storey, Moorfield, *Charles Sumner* (American Statesmen Series). Boston, 1900.

Ticknor, George, *Life, Letters and Journals*, ii vols. Boston, 1876.

Underwood, Francis H., *James Russell Lowell*. Boston, 1882.

"Warrington" Pen Portraits, edited by Mrs. W. S. Robinson. Boston, 1877.

White, Andrew D., *Autobiography*, ii vols. New York, 1907.

Wilson, Henry, *History of the Rise and Fall of the Slave Power in America*, iii vols. Boston, 1872.

——, *History of the Anti-Slavery Measures of the Thirty-seventh and Thirty-eighth United States Congresses* (1865-1868). Hartford, 1868.

Winthrop, Robert C., Jr., *A Memoir of Robert C. Winthrop*. Boston, 1897.

VITA

THE writer was born in New York City, was prepared for college at the Girls' Latin School of Baltimore, and was graduated an A. B. in 1905 from Goucher College, having majored in history under Professor Eleanor L. Lord. In 1908 she received the degree of A. M. from Columbia University. From 1908–1910 she taught history in the High School of Somerville, New Jersey, attending, during the year 1909–1910, a course in American History, at New York University, given by Professor John Spencer Bassett. For the years 1910–1912 as Fellow in History at Smith College she studied Nineteenth Century History, American and European, under Professor John Spencer Bassett and Professor Charles Downer Hazen, and collected much of the data for her dissertation. During the year 1912–1913 she held the John B. Van Meter Fellowship from Goucher College, and completed, in residence at Columbia University, the course requirements for the degree of Doctor of Philosophy under Professors William A. Dunning, Herbert L. Osgood, William S. Shepherd, James Harvey Robinson, Franklin H. Giddings and Henry Johnson, attending also the seminar of Professor Dunning. In 1914 she was appointed Instructor in History at Smith College.